POSTBAG FROM PALESTINE

Postbag from Palestine

Diane Walker

Illustrated by Jane Taylor

eagle

Eagle
Guildford, Surrey

British Library Cataloguing in Publication Data. A catalogue record for this book is available from the British Library.

Published by Eagle, an imprint of Inter Publishing Service (IPS) Ltd, St Nicholas House, 14 The Mount, Guildford, Surrey GU2 5HN.

Phototypeset by Intype, London.
Printed by L.E.G.O., Italy

ISBN: 0 86347 142 0

DEDICATION

To my husband Robin, with thanks for his patience and support during the preparation of this book and always.

ACKNOWLEDGEMENTS

The author gratefully acknowledges the continual help and encouragement given by Margaret and Trevor Cooling in the preparation of this manuscript: some indebtedness lies beyond adequate expression. My thanks also go to Trevor Cooling for the Foreword he has written for the book.

I also wish to thank Fairfield Primary School, Stapleford, for their co-operation and help in enabling me to trial this material. I am grateful to them and to other schools in Stapleford for enabling me to trial the Assembly material in this book.

Final responsibility for the accuracy of the manuscript lies, of course, with the author alone.

This book contains a series of written messages, ranging from letters to bills, wanted posters to invitations. Some are modern means of communication, such as faxes and newspapers. We do not know which methods were in common use in biblical times, and some are obviously anachronistic. But, given humanity's need to communicate news and beliefs in all ages, I feel justified in appropriating all of these methods for this book, for the sake of immediacy and interest.

CONTENTS

FOREWORD

In 1993 Lorna Crossman, a lecturer at St Martin's College, Lancaster, published a short but fascinating report[1] which documented the experience of her PGCE primary students on teaching practice. They found that, even where RE was a neglected subject, Bible stories were still a prevalent feature of the curriculum. However these students also found that the approach adopted by most schools to teaching them was generally unimaginative. The comments of two students on their teaching practice in schools effectively sum up the experience of the whole group:

'Read Bible story, shortened it, children wrote it and coloured in a picture' (page 21).

'Bible story – discuss – write it in books – very traditional . . . and very boring' (page 26).

Such comments should not be read as condemning the use of Bible stories in the primary school. On the contrary, the Bible must have a central and significant place in the primary school RE programme. It is, after all, the central text for Christians, and children will not develop an informed understanding of Christianity if they do not meet Bible stories in RE. Any topic on Christianity, be it covering festivals, beliefs, ethics, community life, Jesus or worship, to name but a few, will include reference to them.

It is not surprising therefore to find that biblical material figures very strongly in the Model RE syllabuses for England published by the School Curriculum and Assessment Authority; in the core RE curriculum for Northern Ireland schools and in the 5–14 RE guidelines published by the Scottish Office Education Department. What is at issue however is the quality of teaching and learning that is being achieved when the Bible is used as part of the primary school curriculum. In considering improving this there are a number of issues that have to be addressed.

The Use of Bible Stories

One clear conclusion from the St Martin's report is that more creative approaches to teaching Bible stories are necessary if they are to be used effectively in school. In particular, children need activities which go beyond simply regurgitating a story in written or drawn form. What is needed are activities that encourage children to interact with the stories in a way that makes demands on their imagination and enables them to appreciate the significance of the issues and themes which the stories explore.

In a major report on Religious Education published in 1994 by the Office for Standards in Education,[2] the author commented that:

'The best teaching incorporated an interesting variety of tasks and allowed time for the pupils to discuss and ask questions about the subject matter in order to understand the religious significance of the focus of study.' (page 12)

Diane Walker has, in this book, provided a unique resource for teachers which gives the tools required to achieve the quality of teaching praised by Ofsted. The innovative postbag, from which comes, amongst others, postcards, letters, diary entries and faxes, offers a range of material to engage children's attention. These are complemented by activities which encourage the exploration of the story. In addition helpful questions are included which stimulate conversations on both 'why' questions, where the significance of the story is discussed, and 'so what' questions, where children's understanding of its relevance and application can be developed. Finally, and importantly, reflections are included which give children a thought to take away and 'chew on' as a result of their encounter with the story. These offer a very powerful tool to ensure that Bible stories are not just information that is gathered by the children, but are a stimulus to their spiritual, moral, social and cultural development.

Issues for Education

It has, however, to be recognised that using the Bible in an imaginative and creative way like this does pose some challenges for teachers. Those questions of particular significance are:

1) *Will not introducing imaginary elements into Bible stories confuse children?*
There is a long tradition in children's literature of using fictitious characters to explore historical events and important themes. It is a device which stimulates thinking and improves understanding, enabling children to draw on the meaning of the story. Children are quite able to cope with this as a device without getting confused, as long as the teacher helps them to distinguish between the imaginative element which is introduced for the purposes of teaching and the story itself as recorded in the Bible. Constant reminders as to the need to make this distinction appear throughout this book.

2) *Is it right to teach the Bible as though it is true?*
From the teacher's point of view this is probably one of the most challenging questions to be faced. Of course it does not just apply to the Bible but to the use of material from any religion in the classroom. In dealing with it there are a number of important principles to bear in mind:

a) It is not the job of the school to tell children what they should believe. Therefore, it is a fundamental principle that no religious material is taught in a way that takes away children's freedom of belief. They should not feel pressurised.
b) On the other hand it is also important that children appreciate the significance of Bible stories for Christians. They therefore need to appreciate that, for Christians, these stories are of a different order from, for example, Grimm's fairy stories. Bible stories both convey truth of a profound kind and, for many Christians, are also true in the sense of actually having happened.
c) In order to clarify the question of truth, it will be important to begin to explore, as appropriate, the different types of literature there are in the Bible. The truth of a piece of poetry like a Psalm is, for example, of a different nature from an account of a historical incident like the crucifixion, or of a parable like the Good Samaritan. They

all convey deep truths in the sense that they teach Christians something about God. However, in the case of the parable and the poem the issue of whether they describe incidents that actually happened is largely irrelevant, whereas that is most certainly not the case with the crucifixion accounts. Children should be encouraged to begin to explore how the question of truth is tied up with the type of literature any given Bible story might be.

d) Probably the most contentious type of stories are those that describe miracles. There is a widespread assumption that these somehow contradict the laws of nature and cannot therefore be believed. This is a complex issue that cannot be dealt with here. An important point to note is that there are many eminent scientists and other distinguished academics who believe that miracles can happen.[3] To tell children they cannot is to pass on the scepticism which is characteristic of Western society. To be fair in our representation of Christianity it is important that children understand that many Christians do believe that the events took place as described in the Bible.

It is important however that miracles are treated in the way the Bible treats them. To give children the impression that Jesus, or other Bible characters, were magicians or wizards who used their powers to gain personal benefit or to fulfil fleeting whims would be to distort the way the Bible records these stories. Rather, they are recorded to illustrate the message of the biblical text. They are not simply extraordinary happenings with no deeper theological significance.

e) Perhaps the single most effective way to ensure that children are both free to come to their own conclusions and yet appreciate that, for Christians, the stories are true, is to employ what has been called owning and grounding language. This simply means that the stories are introduced with phrases like 'we are now going to look at a story that is important for Christians', which emphasises that the story is 'owned' by the Christian community and is 'grounded' in the particular set of beliefs that characterise that community. Such language emphasises the point that the stories are of considerable importance and significance without implying that the children are *required* to believe them. It allows children to reflect on the meaning these stories have for them and what they can learn from them without their feeling pressurised by the assumption that they ought to believe them.

3) *Will not teaching Bible stories lead children to ask questions I cannot answer?*

The short answer is probably yes. Indeed I would go as far as to say, hopefully, yes! Successful teaching will inevitably lead children to probe and to ask searching questions. In the religious realm this will often mean questions like 'was Jesus a loser?' to which there is no easy answer. In seeking to respond to these, the following pointers may provide some help:

a) The purpose of religious education should not be to give children trite answers which have a short sell-by date. Certainly these will often offer temporary satisfaction, but as they get older children will realise that they do not stand the test and will reject them and possibly the religious dimension altogether. Rather, the purpose of religious education is to provide pupils with the tools that they will need for handling deep and complex issues in life. Encouraging exploration through probing questions and

persisting in the struggle to find a way through these is an attitude of mind that will stand children in good stead in a way that simplistic, but easily given, answers will not.
b) Honesty is always the best policy. As teachers, we should never be afraid to admit to our own beliefs and doubts. Children can sense very quickly when they are being given an answer that lacks authenticity. However, honesty also means that we ensure children are aware of the beliefs and doubts of others as well. This is a balance which helps children to realise that difference of opinion over difficult questions is 'OK'.
c) Difficult questions should always be affirmed as valuable and important. Saying, 'That's a very important question and people down the ages have struggled with it' is an important affirmation for a child that finding things puzzling is an integral part of understanding. The modern world is one in which people easily assume that a good question must have a right answer. I think my lecturer who, at the beginning of my first ever philosophy lecture, said, 'If you aren't confused, you haven't understood' was much closer to the truth. The educated person is someone who is challenged by the great mysteries of life, not someone who has all the textbook answers.
d) Finally, children should be encouraged to seek a variety of perspectives. Use their questions as a launching pad for investigative work. This should certainly include getting them to reflect on their own questions by turning them back on them in a different form. 'What makes you think Jesus might have been a loser? What more would we have to know about Jesus to be able to answer your question?' This approach should also widen the field of enquiry to other people. 'What do the rest of the class think? Why don't they ask someone at home? Is there someone from the Christian church we can ask for their opinion?' No doubt this will produce some demanding classroom work. But, in terms of achieving quality of learning, it will be in a different league from the approach of 'write out the story and draw a picture'.[4]

The psychologist Jerome Bruner once wrote a book called *Beyond the Information Given*. His title encapsulates the concern for quality in teaching and learning which is an important feature of modern education. Diane Walker's book offers teachers the tools necessary to go beyond the information given when teaching Bible stories.

Trevor Cooling
Stapleford, Nottingham
May 1995.

Notes

1. Lorna Crossman, 'Salvation Through Schools? A Report and Reflection on Trainee-teacher attitudes to RE' (St Martin's College, 1993).
2. Ofsted 'Religious Education and Collective Worship: 1992–1993' (HMSO, 1994).
3. For further discussion of this issue see: Michael Poole, *A Guide to Science and Belief* (Lion, 1994).
4. For further discussion of this issue see: John Hull *God-talk with Young Children* (Christian Education Movement, 1991).

INTRODUCTION

This book consists of a series of units on key episodes from Jesus' life and teaching. Each unit contains a Bible passage, retold in appropriate language, and a series of questions and activities providing a variety of approaches to the story. Each unit opens with a 'fictional' piece of writing, told by or relating to the biblical characters and events in the story. Its aim is to encourage the children to realise that Bible stories involve people like them, with hopes and worries, work and interests: and to explore how Jesus made a difference to those people's lives. The questions and the assemblies can be used with children to explore the Christian belief that Jesus still makes a difference in people's lives today.

Typical Unit Breakdown

First Section

The opening section takes the form of a piece of writing – a notice, a diary, or a letter, for instance. This is fictional but based on a character or event in the Bible story. It is written usually by a minor participant in the story, or by an eye-witness. A note will make it clear to the children which characters have been 'made up', and which are in the actual Bible story. Its aim is to provide an unusual angle on the story, to help the children to explore the reactions of people at the time, and to explore the significance of the story, by increasing its immediacy. Methods of writing time and dates have been modernised.

Questions

These explore the content of the story and of the first section. The answer to each question could be found in either the first section or in the story, or in both. These questions could be answered by pupils working alone, or with the help of the teacher.

Activity

This section contains a longer activity based on the subject matter of the extracts or on their theme. It involves a variety of activities, including art and drama. Groups of pupils could work on some of these.

Second Section

This starts with the retold Bible Story, accompanied by a large full colour illustration.

Third Section

Background Information

This consists of brief notes for the use of the teacher. It aims to provide them with the information they require to help the children tackle the questions and conversation points. Not all of its information needs to be given to the children, and it cannot answer all the possible queries that teachers and children might have!

Conversation

This section seeks to stimulate a range of subjects for conversation. There is no need to use every suggestion. Nor is it by any means an exhaustive list of possible issues the children will raise. They may well raise issues that are not dealt with – here or in the Background Information. Teachers should not worry if this happens! If the children do ask questions which you feel, for any reason, you cannot answer, this can be taken as an opportunity to explore the issue together. It might lead to an opportunity to invite someone in from the local community to speak to the children, or to answer their questions. The class could find out if they could write to a person or to an organisation with their questions. Not knowing all the answers is not a failure. Several of the stories do raise issues that are difficult to handle. There are notes about these in the appropriate sections, and the general Introduction contains guidance. These Conversation questions are designed to stimulate discussion, not to reach a pre-ordained answer. The children should be encouraged to share their own ideas, but should not feel impelled to do so, or to reach agreement with anyone else. The questions come in a variety of forms. Some are content-based; others ask the children to reflect on the meaning of an incident or of a person's actions: some require an evaluative answer – 'Do you think. . . ?'

Reflection

The purpose of this section should be made very clear to the children from the outset. It is an opportunity for private reflection on the relevant issue: no one will require an account from them of what they were thinking. Of course, some may choose to share with others, but no one must feel impelled to do so. This is their chance to consider the application of the story for themselves.

Assembly

In an Appendix there are suggestions of assemblies that would tie in with the themes of the sections. Most of these could be used independently, too. I have tried to allow for differences in time allotted to assemblies. Most of them involve the children in some way. If an assembly follows a class study of a section, then the children's work on that section could be incorporated into the assembly. Each assembly ends with a:

Prayer or Reflection

Sometimes, a choice of both is offered. The children should not be expected to join in with the prayer and its 'Amen' automatically. It should be made plain that the leader is going to say a prayer: the children's respectful silence is asked for. It is explained that 'Amen' will be said at the end, and they should be given the opportunity to join in with it or not – as they choose.

Photocopiable Pages

All material in this book, both text and images, is fully photocopiable.

Health and Safety

As with any activity in the classroom, the safety of the children must be paramount. Care should be taken for example with potential allergy-triggering substances, and the use of paints and adhesives. Any branches used should be from safe plants, cut in pruning. Teachers are referred to their Health and Safety Guidelines.

Anti-Semitism

It is easy, by careless use of language, to give the impression that Jesus was the enemy of all Jews, who were united in their opposition of him. In fact, he himself was a Jew, living in a Jewish home, choosing Jews as his important first disciples, and relying on the help and bravery of many Jews as he worked. Only a relatively small faction of Jews opposed him and his followers. This should be made clear to the children throughout. Jesus' enemies opposed him for many reasons: racial hatred was not one of them.

ONE

KING IN A STABLE

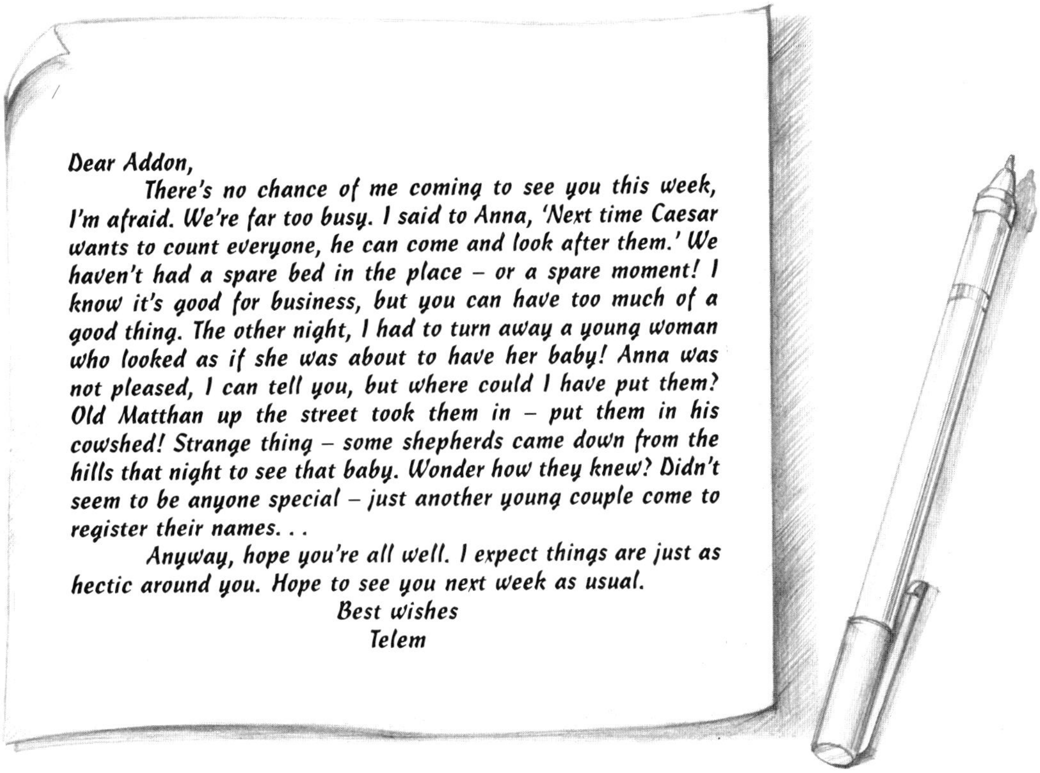

Dear Addon,

There's no chance of me coming to see you this week, I'm afraid. We're far too busy. I said to Anna, 'Next time Caesar wants to count everyone, he can come and look after them.' We haven't had a spare bed in the place – or a spare moment! I know it's good for business, but you can have too much of a good thing. The other night, I had to turn away a young woman who looked as if she was about to have her baby! Anna was not pleased, I can tell you, but where could I have put them? Old Matthan up the street took them in – put them in his cowshed! Strange thing – some shepherds came down from the hills that night to see that baby. Wonder how they knew? Didn't seem to be anyone special – just another young couple come to register their names. . .

Anyway, hope you're all well. I expect things are just as hectic around you. Hope to see you next week as usual.

Best wishes

Telem

Questions

1. How did Mary first learn that she was going to have a baby?

2. How was this baby going to be special?

3. Can you suggest how Joseph felt when he could only find a stable for them to stay in?

Activity

In his letter, Telem the innkeeper says that he is puzzled about the shepherds. Perhaps he met one of them later and asked them what had happened. The conversation could start like this. (We'll call the shepherd Hattil.)

TELEM: You were one of those shepherds the other night weren't you? Why did you leave your sheep?

HATTIL: We were told to!

TELEM: What do you mean?

Continue the conversation until Telem knows everything that happened that night.

NOTE: the shepherds are in the Bible story – but we do not know their real names. Mary and Joseph did fail to find room at the inn, but we do not know if there was an innkeeper, or what his name was if he existed.

King in a Stable

The night was cold and the streets crowded. But here in the stable, the air was warm and still and all was quiet – so quiet that Mary could hear quite plainly the snuffling breath of her son as he lay snugly in the hay-filled trough beside her. It was over – the long, rough journey, the desperate search for somewhere to rest, and the birth of her child. She thought about that day, all those months ago, when an angel – one of God's special messengers – had come to see her! 'You will have a child,' he told her. 'You will call him Jesus. He will be a special child, God's own son.' But he's just a baby, she thought now as she watched Jesus sleeping, my precious baby, but just a baby. How difficult it was to understand! But she believed all that the angel had said: this baby, lying in a borrowed cowshed in an animals' feeding trough was very special!

There was a knock on the door. She thought it might be the inn-keeper's wife returning, but it wasn't. A group of men came in, slowly and hesitantly. She realised they were shepherds. What were they doing here? Did they use this shelter? They were looking at the baby!

They had been out on the hillside as usual, they said, guarding their sheep through the cold, dark night. Suddenly, their little camp was flooded with dazzling light. Someone had spoken to them out of the light, telling them that God's special king had been born and was lying in a stable down in Bethlehem. They had realised that this was an angel, with a message for them. Then other angels had joined him, singing a song of praise to God. And here they were, doing as the angel had told them, worshipping this newborn baby.

After they had left, Mary considered everything that had happened. She had thought that God had told only Joseph and herself about this child. But he had shared the secret with these shepherds, too, sending them to welcome him into the world. She wondered if God would send anybody else to see Jesus. Would other people always know that he was special? It was strange, she decided. Here she was, a young mother with her first baby, far from home in a strange town, forced to sleep in an animal shelter and to lay her son in a trough. 'And yet I feel safe and cared for!' she thought. 'Joseph is so good, and now God has shown us that he

knows just where we are. He is pleased, too – so pleased that he has had to tell others about the beginning of his great plan.'

As she settled down to sleep, her thoughts were full of pictures of the small house waiting for them back in Nazareth. It wouldn't be long before she could take her son back home.

(This story can be found in Matthew 1:18–25 and Luke 1:26–38 and 2:1–20.)

Background Information

Stable/manger: At this time, the poorer people lived in very simple houses consisting of one room. Part of this would be a raised area on which the family lived and slept. Animals were often kept in the lower section, or brought into it at night. Jesus may have been born in such a house therefore, or he may have been born in a rough wooden shelter or in a cave used either just for the animals, or shared by the family. The use of a trough or manger would not necessarily be unusual, therefore. Babies often slept in a sort of hammock suspended from a beam or slung between two poles. At birth, babies were washed, rubbed with salt, and wrapped in a blanket. Strips of cloth ('swaddling-bands') were bound tightly around this. It was thought that this helped the baby's bones to grow strong and straight. The baby was often unwrapped, of course! Some mothers are still advised to wrap new babies securely, to give them a feeling of security.

Census: The order to hold a census came from the Roman Emperor. Each man had to return to the home of his ancestors to enrol for taxation purposes. Joseph traced his descent from King David, so he had to go to David's home village of Bethlehem. (Christians see Micah 5:2 as a prophecy of this.)

Shepherds: The keeping of sheep for their provision of wool was a vital part of the economy. But hired shepherds themselves were not highly regarded, despite their hard, dangerous work. God's choice of shepherds as witnesses to the arrival of his Son stresses the fact that Jesus came to help everyone, whatever their social standing.

Inns: We do not know if there were any formal inns in Bethlehem. It was only a small village. It seems likely that the 'inns' were private homes opened by their custom of hospitality to friends and travellers alike.

Conversation

A. Why were Mary and Joseph in a stable?

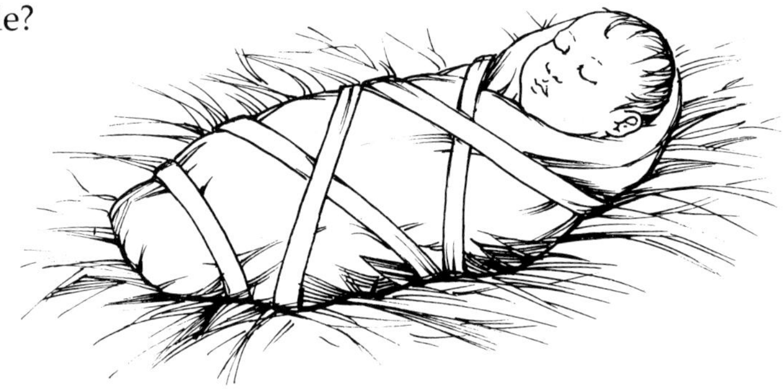

B. People had been waiting for God's special king for hundreds of years.
Is a stable the sort of place in which they would have expected him to be born? Where would they have expected him to be born? Christians believe that Jesus was that special king.

C. Jesus was born in a stable or a poor family's house, cared for by ordinary, poor parents. Christians believe that this was not an accident, or a mistake, but a deliberate choice by God. Why do you think it is important to Christians that Jesus was born into an ordinary family and not to a rich, royal family?

Reflection

One of Jesus' names is Emmanuel. This means, 'God with us' – God's son sharing the ups and downs of life. Would Christians feel this was true if Jesus had lived a safe, comfortable life?

TWO

CHRISTMAS PRESENTS!

WANTED

For withholding vital information from the King!
Three wealthy foreigners. Last seen leaving King Herod's palace.
Believed to be heading for Bethlehem. . .

REWARD OFFERED FOR INFORMATION LEADING TO THEIR ARREST.

Apply in person to Chief Security Office, The Palace, Jerusalem.

Questions

1. Why had the travellers started on their journey?

2. Why did they go to Herod's palace?

3. Herod lied to them. Why did he really want to find Jesus?

Activity

The wise men brought gifts of gold, frankincense and myrrh. What sort of containers do you think they would have used? Would Mary and Joseph have been able to guess what was inside from the outside of the packaging?
Choose one of the gifts. Design packaging for it that would reflect the contents and their meaning.

Christians believe that Jesus came as a 'disguised package' – the Son of God as a helpless baby.

Christmas Presents!

The star was still there, still shining brightly ahead of them! The travellers could see it clearly as they came out of Herod's palace. 'Look!' one of them said. 'We were wrong! The star wasn't leading us here to Jerusalem. We still haven't reached the right place.' Forgetting their weariness, they set off once more, heading for the star.

That star! They had followed it for so long now. At times they thought they would never reach the end of their journey. Months ago, they had seen it for the first time, its light blazing, outshining the stars they studied each night. They were clever men, all of them, and had studied many books. They knew what this star meant. 'A great king has been born! We must go to him!' A king whose birth was announced in the sky was a special king indeed! They were rich men, too; rich enough to buy suitable gifts for such a king and to make such a long journey to they knew not where.

But when they reached Jerusalem, they had forgotten about the star for a while. This was the city where the King of Judea lived: the new king must be here. So they went to the palace, and asked King Herod where the new king was. Herod did not know where he was, but his advisers did. Yes, they said, as Herod knew, the Jews had been waiting for years for a special king. This must be the one. They told him where he would be born. Herod was worried. He was King in Judea. No one else must be allowed to set himself up as king! Somehow, he must get rid of this 'king'! He thought of a plan. He told the travellers where the king was, and sent them away with false promises. 'Come back and tell me when you have found him. For I, too, want to visit such a great king.'

But the travellers did not know about Herod's true intentions as they stood on a hill overlooking the small village of Bethlehem. 'Look – it's obvious where we have to go,' one of them was saying. 'See that small building over there? The star is directly over it!' They hurried down and knocked eagerly on the door. At last they had reached the king!

Joseph opened the door and gazed in amazement at the richly-dressed travellers standing there. What were they doing here? They greeted him, and said, 'We have come to see the King.' Now Joseph understood. He led them in, and there was Mary, nursing her son. The travellers knelt before them. So this was the King they had travelled to see – no queen's son, in a luxurious palace, but the child of an ordinary young woman, living in an ordinary poor house!

Strange gifts they had brought for such a child! There was gold for the king they had come to see. One brought frankincense, and Mary and Joseph recognised its fragrance from the Temple. And there was myrrh. Mary was puzzled. Myrrh was used in burials: what a strange gift to give to a child whose life was just beginning! But she thanked the travellers, and listened to their story. What a long way they had come, just to see Jesus! She marvelled at the way in which God had told them about Jesus, and had led them safely all this way!

But later, God warned the travellers of the danger threatening his young King, speaking to them in their sleep. 'You must not return home through Jerusalem,' he told them. 'Herod wants to hurt this child. Go home another way secretly!'

So the travellers set off, making sure that they stayed a long way from Jersualem. Soon, Mary and Joseph left Bethlehem as well with Jesus. God sent them to another country, to Egypt, to be safe while Herod tried to find the baby. Eventually, the family returned to Nazareth, and lived an ordinary life. And the child born in a stable and greeted by angels, shepherds and travellers grew up with his younger brothers and sisters.

(This story can be found in Matthew 2:1–23.)

Background Information

Herod: There are several King Herods in the New Testament! Sorting out who did what and their relationship to each other can be difficult. The Herod at the time of Jesus' birth is known as Herod the Great. He was the builder of the Temple. He was not a popular ruler, however. The Jewish people resented him because he was a client king of their enemies, the Romans. He was not of pure Jewish descent, either. He actually killed some of his own children because they had a better claim to the throne through their mother, who belonged to the ancient ruling house. So his behaviour when he hears of a possible rival king with a better claim is not surprising. One of his sons was King in Judea when Mary and Joseph returned with Jesus from Egypt. They settled in Galilee to avoid him. Later in the New Testament, another one of Herod the Great's sons – Antipas, known as Herod the Tetrarch – imprisoned and killed John the Baptist. It was this Herod who presided at the trial of Jesus. A grandson of Herod the Great – Agrippa 1 – persecuted the early Christians, and his son, another Agrippa, heard Paul's case.

Gold: Gold has always been a symbol of wealth and high-standing. In biblical times too it was a symbol of great worth, associated with the Temple and with the worship of God. For Christians, it represents the kingship of Christ.

Frankincense: This expensive resin was used in the holy anointing oil used in the ceremony of consecrating Israel's priests to their service. It was also used in the worship in the Temple. It represents the priesthood of Christ. A priest was someone who acted to bring God and people closer together.

Myrrh: This, like frankincense, is a resin from trees. It was expensive and rare. It too was used in the anointing oil. It was also used in the embalming and preparation of bodies for burial. The gift of it to Jesus is a sign that he is to die for his people. Interestingly, it sometimes had connotations of joy also, in the Old Testament. Jesus' death, Christians believe, brought joy to many people, because of the good that came out of it.

Conversation

A. Herod had a 'hidden agenda' when he spoke to the travellers. This means that he was lying about what he intended to do. He was 'using' them. Can you think of any way in which we can use people like this, to get something done that we do not want to do or can't be bothered to do?
B. What 'gifts' did Mary and Joseph give to Jesus? Not all gifts are visible!
C. Discuss what the travellers' three gifts meant. What do you think that Mary and Joseph thought of them?

Reflection

Gold, frankincense and myrrh were strange gifts to give to a baby! They foreshadowed and foretold events which lay far in his future. Christians believe that Jesus' death on the cross was not an accident or a mistake. They believe that he came to earth in order to do a job: that job included dying.

THREE

LOST IN THE CITY?

Dear Editor,

I have had to complain about the behaviour of today's children before, and I know that my complaints do not make me popular. But what I have seen today proves everything I have said in the past. Children today do not know their place! They have no idea about how to treat their elders and betters!

I went to the Temple today as I always do, to spend time in prayer. And there, actually in the Temple Courts, was a young boy. I'm sure he was only just thirteen, if that! He was discussing things with the teachers. Discussing things, mind - not just listening respectfully, but offering his own opinions as if anyone wanted to hear them! Then his parents came rushing in. They'd 'lost' him, would you believe! Out of control, that's what he was!

Yours,

Indignant of Jerusalem

Questions

1. Why had Mary and Joseph gone to Jerusalem?

2. It seems strange to us that they didn't realise Jesus wasn't with them. Why didn't they miss him earlier in the day?

3. How would Mary and Joseph feel as they searched for and found their son?

Activity

The writer of the letter obviously did not approve of Jesus behaving in this way! Write an answering letter as if it is from one of the Teachers who were enjoying their conversation with Jesus.

NOTE: Indignant of Jerusalem is, of course, an imaginary person.

Lost in the City?

The Passover Feast had finished. Early the next morning, Mary and Joseph set off home with their friends and relatives from Nazareth. They travelled steadily all day. Jesus didn't join them for the meal at midday, but they weren't worried. He had spent most of the journey to Jersualem with his cousins and friends and was probably with them now. He'd turn up when he was hungry or sleepy. So, by the time they realised that he was not with anyone in the party, they had come a long way from Jerusalem, and faced a long, worrying walk back.

All the way, they kept asking themselves questions. What was Jesus doing? Was he all right? Who was he with? Had he somehow lost the group on the way, or was he still in Jerusalem? But they could find no answers. All they could do was ask God to look after Jesus, and to guide them to him.

It took three days of weary searching before they found Jesus at last. By then, Mary was sure he must be ill or hurt. Or perhaps he had been kidnapped! She couldn't help but think of the danger from the King he had been in as a baby. Was this King frightened of him, too? Had he somehow traced them? Where was Jesus?

Then, when they did find him, he was all right – perfectly all right and enjoying himself, even! He was sitting in the Temple Courts, listening to some of the Teachers who worked there. He was even asking questions, and discussing things with these learned men! Hadn't he even missed his mother? Didn't he realise – or care – how worried they had been?

Mary's fear and her relief and joy at finding him spilled over into anger. 'Jesus!' she said. 'How could you do this to us? We've been searching everywhere! I was sure you were hurt or lost at least!'

Jesus was surprised. 'I'm sorry,' he told them, 'but I thought you'd know where I was. I thought you'd realise I'd be here, in my Father's house.'

What could Mary say? She could not argue with this boy: this was his Father's house! 'But I'm still his mother,' she thought. 'How else will he confuse me as he grows up?'

They set off home for Nazareth again – this time with Jesus! And he was just as he had always been: their eldest son, keen to help and learn, to eat and to play – just a normal boy growing up in Nazareth.

(This story can be found in Luke 2:41–52.)

Background Information

Temple Courts: The great Temple built by Herod had several Courts, or areas, around the inner Holy Place. The outer one was the Court of the Gentiles. As its name indicates, even non-Jews were allowed in this Court. Then came the Court of the Women, in which Jews of either sex were allowed. Jesus did some of his teaching here. Then the next Court was only accessible to Jewish men: this was the Court of Israel. Groups of teachers – or Rabbis – taught their followers in the Courts. They were the Scribes, a group of educated men once responsible for copying the Law, as their name suggests. During the Exile of the Jewish people, the Scribes became responsible for recording and passing on the oral law. This was the accumulated knowledge and traditions of the Elders. By this time, teaching had become their main responsibility. They used the method of teaching by argument. Jesus joined a group of these students.

Temple: The Temple was the spiritual centre of Israel. Pilgrims flocked to Jerusalem at the times of the great festivals, especially the Passover.

Passover: This was the Jewish year's most important festival. It was held – and still is held in Jewish homes around the world – to remember and to celebrate the night when God 'passed over' the Jewish homes in Egypt when the first-born sons of the Egyptians died. This was the night when Moses finally led the people out of slavery.

An old street in Jerusalem near the Temple

Conversation

A. The Bible points out that Jesus grew up 'obedient to them' (to Mary and Joseph.) Do you think Jesus is deliberately disobeying them here, or do you think he had another reason for his action?

B. We don't know a lot about Jesus' childhood. What does this episode tell us about him?

C. Many people – including children – are put off going to church because of the way some chuches expect people to behave. How do you think people should behave in churches? Why do people go to church?

Reflection

Jesus here had a conflict of loyalties. It was one situation in which it was difficult to please his Father (God) and his parents. We can find ourselves in similar situations, in which different people expect different things from us. Often talking will help solve the problem. Can you think of any such problems you have faced or are facing?

FOUR

'THIS IS MY SON!'

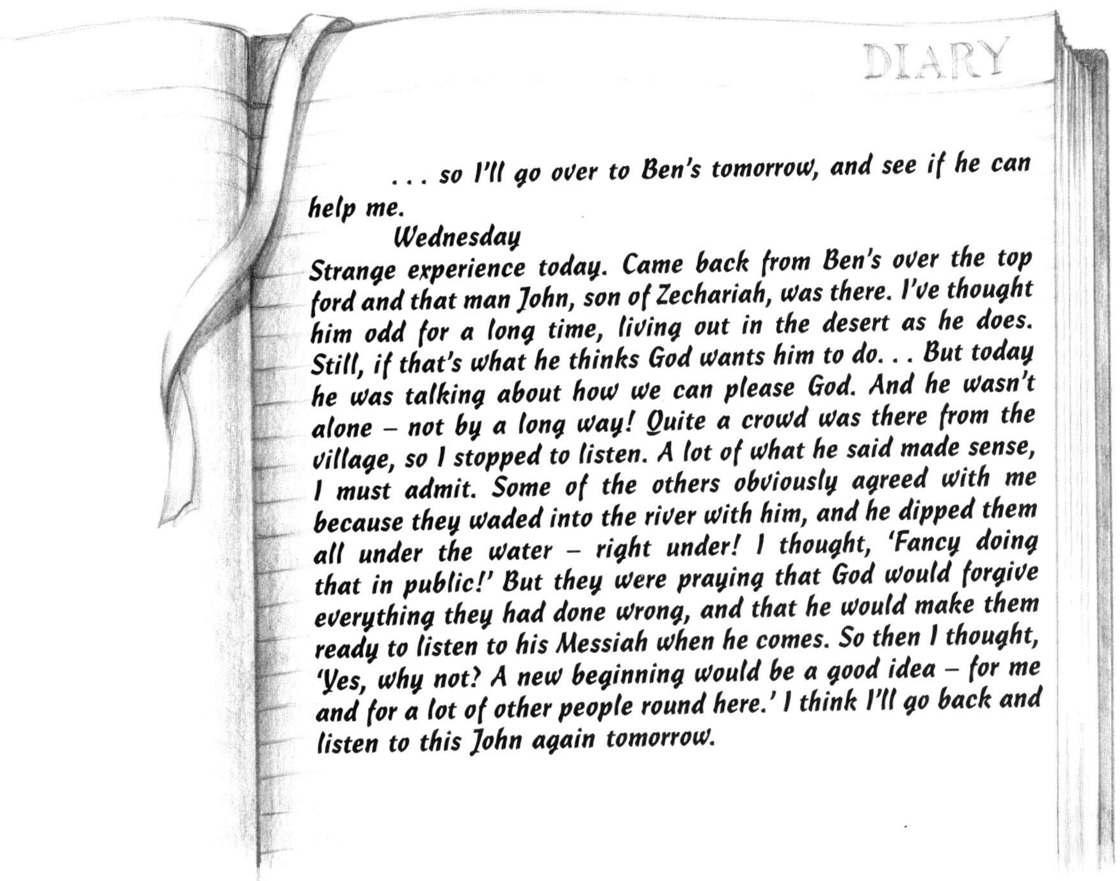

DIARY
. . . so I'll go over to Ben's tomorrow, and see if he can help me.
Wednesday
Strange experience today. Came back from Ben's over the top ford and that man John, son of Zechariah, was there. I've thought him odd for a long time, living out in the desert as he does. Still, if that's what he thinks God wants him to do. . . But today he was talking about how we can please God. And he wasn't alone – not by a long way! Quite a crowd was there from the village, so I stopped to listen. A lot of what he said made sense, I must admit. Some of the others obviously agreed with me because they waded into the river with him, and he dipped them all under the water – right under! I thought, 'Fancy doing that in public!' But they were praying that God would forgive everything they had done wrong, and that he would make them ready to listen to his Messiah when he comes. So then I thought, 'Yes, why not? A new beginning would be a good idea – for me and for a lot of other people round here.' I think I'll go back and listen to this John again tomorrow.

Questions

1. Why were the people at the river?

2. What was John's message to them?

3. John did not want to baptise Jesus at first. Why not?

Activity

The writer of the diary says that he is going back to listen to John the next day. Write the entry for Thursday, imagining that this was the day on which Jesus came to John to be baptised. Describe what you saw at the river.

NOTE: The diary writer and Ben are not people out of the Bible story.

'This is My Son!'

In the mornings, the people hurried out from Jerusalem and from all the villages around. Some had already heard John teaching and wanted to hear more. Others had been told about him by their friends and were eager to hear his message for themselves. Some just wanted to find out what all the fuss was about. All of them gathered on the bank of the river and waited.

John did not look like their teachers in the synagogues and the Temple! His clothes were made of camel's hair, and people said that he had lived alone for years, out in the desert, eating locusts and honey. He had spent his life listening and talking to God, finding out what God wanted him to say. Now, day after day, he taught them, explaining that something wonderful was about to happen.

'Our people have been waiting for years for God's special leader, the Messiah, to come to us. Soon now – very soon – we will see him. But we are not ready to meet him. We are not living as God wants us to live. We break God's rules and do things that upset him every day. We need to realise that we are not perfect and to say sorry to him for these things. And we need to promise to try never to do them again.'

Many of the people agreed with John. They realised they needed to be forgiven. John prayed with them as they asked God to forgive them and to help them in the future. Then, John led them into the River Jordan. He dipped them right under the water, holding them safely.

'This washing in the river, this baptism, is a sign that you are forgiven. God has washed you clean of all the things you did wrong. Now you can start again and look forward to meeting the Messiah.'

So, day after day, the people flocked to hear John, and many were baptised. But one day someone special came to John. It was Jesus! As soon as John saw him, he knew that this was God's Son, the Messiah. And Jesus was asking John to baptise him! 'I am not fit even to be your servant, Lord!' John protested.

But Jesus insisted. 'You must baptise me today, John,' he told him. 'This has to happen.'

So Jesus was baptised by John in the River Jordan. And, as he straightened up out of the water, a dove appeared, hovering over his head. And God's voice said, 'You are my Son whom I love. I am very pleased with you and with everything you are doing.'

Then John told the people standing around that this was the person he had told them about. This was the special king they had all been waiting for, who had come to earth so that they might live as God's friends.

(This story can be found in Matthew 3:13–17; Mark 1:9–11; Luke 3:21, 22.)

Background Information

Baptism: Different churches today have different beliefs about baptism and its meaning and significance. John the Baptist baptised people to show their awareness of their own sins and their belief that the coming Messiah would forgive these sins and help them to live differently. Jesus came to him for baptism for other reasons. He wanted to ally himself with John's work and show his approval of it; he was dedicating himself to his own work on earth: and it was a sign that he identified with sinful and imperfect humanity, even though Christians believe that he himself was sinless. When the Apostles began the Christian tradition of baptism, obeying Jesus' command to do so, they baptised people to show that they had been forgiven by God, and had entered a new life with the help of the Holy Spirit who now lived in them. Baptism would not have been a new idea to the Jewish people, as it was already established as a symbol of religious purification and consecration. It may have been used too in the rituals involved when a Gentile became a member of the Jewish community, as a proselyte (convert).

Conversation

A. What did John say baptism was? Why did he baptise people?

B. It is not obvious in the text of the Bible whether Jesus alone heard God's voice and saw the dove, or whether Jesus and John heard and saw them, or whether everyone present did! What do you think? (The dove here represents the Holy Spirit to Christians.)

C. We use water for cleaning things in everyday life. We are able to restore and make good things that dirt has spoilt. Some things 'spoil' our lives, such as stealing and rudeness. Can you think of anything else that the people at the River Jordan might have felt was spoiling their lives?

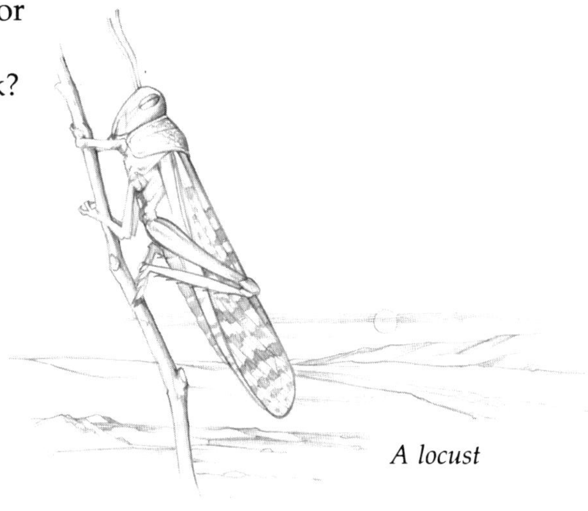

A locust

Reflection

Baptism is a sign of sins forgiven and of a new start to life. Just a new start is not enough, however. It is easy to do wrong things again! We need to be different inside. Christians believe that Jesus can and will help people to change if they ask him to.

FIVE

REAL FRIENDS?

PALESTINE REPORTER

Who's doing what in your region

Rumour has it that the new prophet from Galilee is gathering an increasingly bizarre group of followers around him. His daily companions include a tax-collecter (who probably lined his own purse as well as those of his Roman friends) and a member of a group pledged to rid the country of the Romans at any cost! It will be interesting to see how these two get on with each other!

Also, I am surprised to hear that Jesus' little band of travellers has received financial and practical help from the wife of one of Herod's top servants. I wouldn't want to be in her sandals - or her husband's - if Herod finds out! Jesus does not seem to mind meeting with Samaritans. The whole pack of them frequently eat at the sort of house the rest of us would not like to be seen dead at. There seems to be no part of society with which Jesus is not happy to mix : he does not even avoid lepers!

Now reports are coming in that he has been caught working on the Sabbath. I think we can safely say that Jesus is not very popular at the moment with the people who matter in the country! We await developments with interest.

Questions

1. What sort of life did Jesus and his followers lead?

2. There are a lot of names in this story! Make a list of all the names you can find. Write one fact about each person next to the name. (You will not be able to do this for everyone!) Read your list, and think about how different these people were from each other.

3. Joanna and Nicodemus were secret friends of Jesus. Why did they have to hide their friendship?

Activity

Imagine Joanna's husband has just discovered her friendship with Jesus. Write what he says to her in one speech bubble, and her reply in the other.

Real Friends?

'I want to follow you and be your disciple,' the young man told Jesus. 'I have always tried to obey all God's laws. What else must I do?'

Jesus looked at him. 'You must sell everything you have and give the money to those who need it. Then you can come and join us.'

But the young man shook his head: he couldn't do that. Jesus watched him sadly. It wasn't the man's wealth that had stopped him following Jesus. It was his love of his wealth. The man loved his money more than he loved Jesus. So he went back to his money and his comfortable life.

For life as one of Jesus' followers was neither comfortable nor safe! They travelled through the countryside, far away from home, sometimes sleeping at a friend's house, sometimes outdoors. They were often tired, hungry and cold, and all the time they knew that many of the religious leaders were trying to find reasons to arrest Jesus as he taught and healed in the towns and villages.

But Jesus did have many friends willing to give up their usual lives and

to take risks in order to help him. Jesus looked round at his disciples as they talked to the people who had been listening to him. These were his special friends, the twelve men he had chosen to lead his people after he had returned to heaven. They went everywhere with him, and he taught them as they watched him at work. He caught sight of Judas and sighed. He alone would leave this group, helping Jesus' enemies to arrest him. But the rest would be strong leaders. They were not perfect, of course. They were just ordinary men who had left their ordinary lives to follow him.

Amongst these were the brothers, Andrew and Peter. Peter would, Jesus knew, let him down badly, but he would later become one of the main leaders of his people. Peter and his brother had been fishermen, as had James and John, well-known for their quick tempers. Thomas was there too, and James son of Alphaeus and Thaddaeus, next to the friends Philip and Nathanael. Matthew and Simon had been enemies, not friends, when Jesus brought them into the group. For Matthew had worked for the hated Romans as a tax-collector, and Simon had been working to drive out the Romans! But now all the disciples were learning to work together.

Jesus set off for Jericho, and his disciples – his special followers – joined him. He thought of his other friends. There were Mary, Martha and Lazarus at Bethany and others like them, who were always eager to welcome him and his disciples into their homes. There were other women, too, such as Susanna, Mary Magdala and Joanna, who provided money and food whenever they could. Jesus smiled as he thought of brave Joanna: she was married to one of King Herod's servants. Herod hated Jesus. If he found out, she would be in great danger, so she had to help him secretly. Nicodemus, one of the Jewish leaders, was another secret friend. He came to see Jesus during the night, to keep his visit secret from the other leaders, for they were Jesus' enemies. But soon he would speak out about his friendship with Jesus, along with another secret friend, Joseph of Arimathea: but that would not be until Jesus was dead.

Jesus stopped walking. He looked round at his disciples, these men who had gladly given up everything to follow him. He thought about the future – how his death would leave them confused and lost, and he spoke to them. 'You have been good friends to me and have given up your homes and families these past few years,' he said. 'But anyone who gives up anything because they love and follow me will be repaid many times over by my love and care for them. Remember this now and especially in the future.'

And he walked on towards Jericho and Jerusalem.

(This story can be found in Luke 6:12–16 and 8:1–3.)

Background Information

Matthew: Matthew was a tax-collector for the Romans, and was therefore unpopular with the Jews. See the notes on Zacchaeus, p 56.
Simon: Simon was possibly a member of a group of freedom-fighters, called the Zealots, who were dedicated to removing the Romans from their land. They had not yet reached their full power, but seized on any opportunities to harass the Roman authorities. Simon and Matthew would have been natural enemies because of their political allegiances.
Women: Jesus was unusual in his day because of the status he gave to women. He admitted them into the circle of his friends and naturally included them in his teaching. He would teach in the Women's Court at the Temple so that women could hear him, too. The opinion current at the time was that women could not profit from such teaching.
Lepers: Other skin diseases may have been classed with leprosy. Sufferers were exiled from home, and lived by begging. As the diseases were thought to be highly contagious, most people avoided the lepers.

Jesus also mixed with people the authorities dismissed as 'sinners' and hopeless cases. Jesus' answer was that he had come to help anyone who needed him: these people acknowledged their need, unlike many of the Jewish leaders.
Herod: Herod only reigned with the permission of the Romans. If popular leaders such as Jesus caused unrest, Herod knew that he could lose his position. He would not have approved, therefore, of any support given to Jesus.
Sabbath: The Sabbath was intended by God to be a welcome day of rest. By this time, the Sabbath was hedged in by many petty interpretations of the Sabbath laws. These teachers saw the healings performed by Jesus on the Sabbath as work, and condemned him as a law-breaker because of them.
Samaria: See notes on p 44.

Conversation

A. Talk about 'Gossip Columns' today. Teachers may wish to bring in a Gossip Column from a magazine (choose with care). In the Palestine Reporter's Gossip Column, what is the writer's attitude to Jesus? Which words tell you this?

B. Write each of the disciples' names on a strip of paper, and place them in a box. Take it in turns to draw out a name. Tell the others why you think Jesus chose that man. Sometimes we do not know: can you think of a reason?

C. Most of Jesus' disciples and followers were good friends to him. What qualities made them 'good friends' to Jesus?

Reflection

Do people ever make friends just for what they can get out of the friendship? Real friendship works two ways: friends have to give as well as take.

SIX

WHO IS THIS MAN?

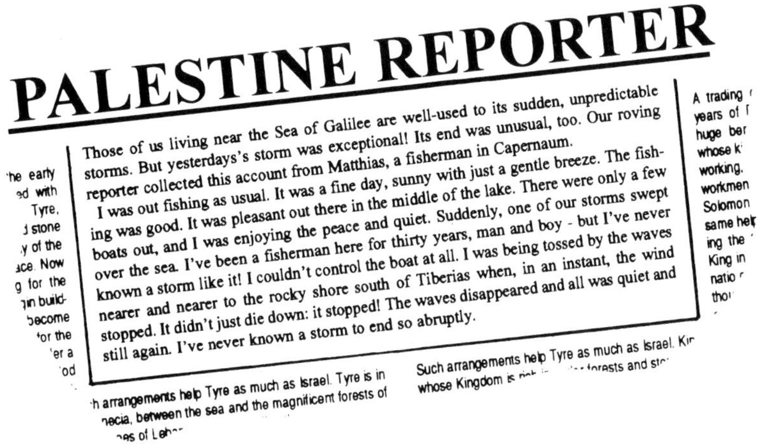

PALESTINE REPORTER

Those of us living near the Sea of Galilee are well-used to its sudden, unpredictable storms. But yesterdays's storm was exceptional! Its end was unusual, too. Our roving reporter collected this account from Matthias, a fisherman in Capernaum.

I was out fishing as usual. It was a fine day, sunny with just a gentle breeze. The fishing was good. It was pleasant out there in the middle of the lake. There were only a few boats out, and I was enjoying the peace and quiet. Suddenly, one of our storms swept over the sea. I've been a fisherman here for thirty years, man and boy - but I've never known a storm like it! I couldn't control the boat at all. I was being tossed by the waves nearer and nearer to the rocky shore south of Tiberias when, in an instant, the wind stopped. It didn't just die down: it stopped! The waves disappeared and all was quiet and still again. I've never known a storm to end so abruptly.

Questions

1. Can you find two reasons why people kept coming to Jesus?

2. Why did Jesus want to cross over the lake?

3. What do you think the disciples expected Jesus to do when they woke him? They were amazed at what he did do!

Activity

Imagine you are one of the disciples in the boat during the storm and/or its calming. Write a poem based on what you are experiencing through your senses (smell, touch, sight, hearing and taste). Here is an example based on Jesus praying in the hills. Notice how each sense is involved.

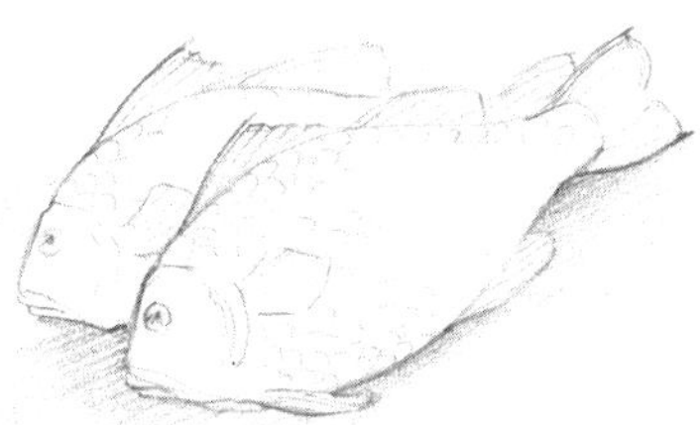

He felt the sharp stones beneath his feet,
He smelt the wild herbs and the fresh wind,
He saw the bare hills and the sparkling water below him,
He tasted the clean, tangy air,
He 'heard' God's voice, and forgot everything else.

Once you have some ideas, you do not have to use all five senses.

NOTE: This fisherman is a made-up character. But we are told that there were other boats out on the water at the same time.

Who is This Man?

Everywhere Jesus went, the crowds gathered. Many people had heard of the wonderful things he had done, and of the illnesses he had cured. Some of them came hoping to be healed themselves or bringing their relatives or friends. Others came to see any miracle he might do. Many came to him because they had heard about his teaching. They sat for hours listening to him because his teaching was exciting, and he gave them information about God and themselves. He used stories about things they knew and

understood to help them understand more about God and his love for them. He talked about lamps spreading light, and about seeds and treasure, builders and fruit trees. And everyone who met him felt that he cared about them – that they mattered to him.

So Jesus was kept very busy. Often, the crowds even interrupted his meals! This was how he wanted it to be: he wanted to help as many people as he could. But all his work and caring for others did make him tired. At times, all he wanted was to go somewhere quiet for a while, to talk with God and to hear what God wanted to say to him. He needed this to help him to continue his work. The hills above Galilee were a good place to go when he needed to. So one day, he asked some of his disciples to take him over the lake in their boat, away from the crowds. And, as they rowed quietly over the calm waters, Jesus fell asleep in the back of the boat.

Suddenly, without any warning, one of Galilee's infamous storms sprang up. The wind roared down from the hills above the water, whipping it up into great crashing waves. The fishermen with Jesus were experienced. They relied on this sea for their livelihood, and they were well used to all its moods. They had weathered many storms, and knew just what to do to be safe. But they soon realised that this storm was different from any they had encountered before. They could not control the boat: and they panicked!

One of them struggled back to where Jesus was still sleeping. 'Master!' he shouted above the wind's howling, roughly shaking him awake. 'We're going to drown! Don't you care?'

Jesus woke up with a start. He realised immediately what was happening, and stood up. He raised his arms, and spoke to the winds: 'Be quiet!' He said to the waves, 'Be still!'

And at once all was peaceful.

He looked at his bedraggled disciples as they gazed at him in amazement. 'Don't you understand?' he asked them. 'Don't you believe in me at all?' He shook his head sadly, and then settled down again to rest.

The disciples were still shocked by all that had happened. 'Who is this man?' they whispered to each other. 'Why, even the winds and the waves do what he tells them!'

And then the little boat carried on over the peaceful water.

(This story can be found in Matthew 8:23–27; Mark 4:35–41; Luke 8:22–25.)

Background Information

Fishing: Nearly all of Israel's fishing was on the Sea of Galilee. Here, fishing supported whole village communities. In fact, one was actually called 'Pickling', as this was where the fish were preserved. So the lake's fishermen were experienced men. The lake is well-known for the suddenness and severity of the storms which sweep across the water from the narrow valleys, acting as wind funnels, on its eastern side.
Miracles: Please see the notes on miracles under 'And now say thank you!'.

Conversation

A. The disciples had seen Jesus perform several miracles by the time this happened. Why was he disappointed in them when they panicked in the storm?

B. Jesus needed some time alone. He used this time to pray. Does everyone need time alone? Why have you given this answer? Some people have too much time alone! What is the difference between being alone by choice and loneliness?

C. Christians believe that the other miracles that Jesus did show that he has power over sickness and death. What does this one show?

Reflection

Jesus puzzled the disciples. They asked 'Who is this man?' This is a question people still ask today. Have you ever met people – or heard of people – who have made you think seriously about things?

SEVEN

'IT'S TOO LATE!'

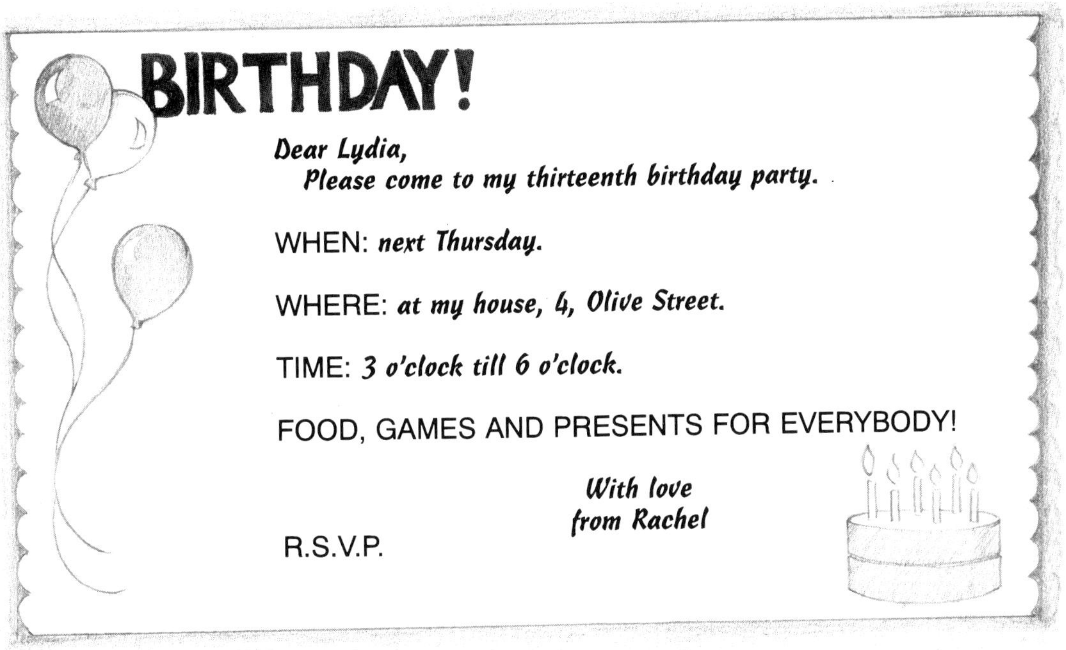

BIRTHDAY!

Dear Lydia,
Please come to my thirteenth birthday party.

WHEN: *next Thursday.*

WHERE: *at my house, 4, Olive Street.*

TIME: *3 o'clock till 6 o'clock.*

FOOD, GAMES AND PRESENTS FOR EVERYBODY!

With love
from Rachel

R.S.V.P.

Questions

1. How old was Jairus' daughter?
2. Why did Jairus go to Jesus?
3. Why did Jesus stop on his way to Jairus' house?

Activity

Jairus and his wife didn't expect to be celebrating their daughter's thirteenth birthday! Imagine you are Jairus. Write the speech you think he would have given at his daughter's party. You can imagine she is called Rachel, and make up a name for your wife if you need one.

NOTE: We do not know what Jairus' daughter's name was really, or her friend's. We are not sure if they would have held a birthday party, even. But we can be sure that their daughter's thirteenth birthday would have been a very special day to them!

'It's Too Late!'

Jairus was an important man. He was one of the rulers of the synagogue at Capernaum. Today he was very worried because his twelve-year-old daughter, whom he loved dearly, was very ill. The doctors had warned her parents that she might die.

Jairus looked down at her as she lay on her bed, so still and quiet. What could he do? He turned to his wife. 'I know,' he said. 'I'll bring Jesus to her! I'm sure he'll be able to help her!' And he rushed out.

Jesus was down by the lake, surrounded by a crowd of people who had come to hear his teaching. Jairus pushed his way through them, and knelt at Jesus' feet. 'My daughter's dying. Please come and help her!' he begged.

Jesus agreed to immediately, and they set off, Jairus showing the way. But they could only go slowly. There were so many people all wanting to stay near Jesus. Jairus became more and more worried. His daughter was dying!

Then Jesus stopped! He looked around him. 'Someone touched me,' he said.

The disciples looked at the crowds. Touched him? Of course someone had touched him! They were all so crowded that they could hardly move! What did he mean?

'The crowd is so great that we can't help bumping into each other,' Peter said.

'No, I don't mean that,' Jesus explained. 'Someone touched me because they needed me to heal them. And they have been healed! Who was it?'

There was silence. Jairus was nearly frantic. Why couldn't they hurry on? What about his daughter?

Then a woman stepped forward. She knelt at Jesus' feet, trembling. 'I touched you, Jesus,' she said, faintly. 'I have been ill for so long, and no one has ever been able to help me. When I heard about you, I knew that you could help me – but I didn't want to take up your time. I'm not worth it. I thought, "If I can just touch, that will be enough." And,' she went on in a stronger voice, 'it was enough. I am healed! Thank you!'

Jesus took her hand and helped her up. 'You have been healed because you believed in me and in my power, not just because you touched me,' he told her. 'Everything is all right now.'

While he was speaking, some men came up to Jairus. 'Don't bother Jesus any longer,' they told Jairus. 'Your daughter is dead. It is too late.'

Jairus was heartbroken. He turned to tell Jesus, but he had heard. 'Don't worry!' he told Jairus. 'Just carry on believing.' He turned to his disciples and chose Peter, James and John to go with him. Then they walked on to Jairus' house.

When they arrived, they could hear the mourners crying. 'The child is not dead,' he told them. 'She is just sleeping.' But they laughed at him. They had seen many dead people before. They knew she was dead! But Jesus insisted they should leave. He and his three disciples went into the

child's room with her parents. Jairus held his breath. What would happen now?

Jesus walked over to the bed. He took her hands and said, 'Young girl, get up!'

And she did! She opened her eyes, and stretched. She smiled at her parents, and got up off the bed and went to them. And they held her and thanked Jesus for this miracle. 'Don't tell anyone about this,' he told them. Then he smiled. 'Your daughter has been ill. I think she's ready for a good meal!' he told her mother. Then he left with his friends.

(This story can be found in Matthew 9:18–26; Mark 5:21–43; Luke 8:40–56.)

Background Information

The woman who was healed: Her town would probably have had a doctor: it may even have had a surgeon! She could have travelled to other doctors, too. But no one had been able to help her.
Ruler of the Synagogue: By this time, there were synagogues in the vast majority of towns and villages, wherever Jewish communities lived. Some towns had more than one. We are told that Jairus was a 'ruler' or 'official' in his local synagogue. He may have been the sole ruler, or a member of the ruling board. The rulers were responsible for keeping order and inviting people to read and speak during the services. He might, therefore, already have asked Jesus to speak at a service.
Mourners: Eastern mourning customs tend to be different from Western customs. Some people tend to avoid or even to be suspicious of loud, open expressions of grief. The Jews would, similarly, doubt the sincerity of mourning which was not obvious and open. It was usual to employ professional mourners to help the family to show their real sorrow and mourning. Musicians were also employed, to play the flute to accompany the funeral processions. In hot countries, a quick burial is advisable. The funerary rites were already under way for Jairus' daughter.
Miracles: Please see the information on miracles under 'And now say thank you!'.

Conversation

A. Why didn't the woman come and ask for help openly as Jairus did? Christians believe that Jesus values everyone, no matter what our opinion is of ourselves.

B. Jesus knew that someone had deliberately touched him because they needed help. He also knew that that person had been healed. He recognised that this person really needed him. Do we recognise people's need or not?

C. Read the invitation to the girl's party once more. This was a birthday that the girl's parents did not expect to be celebrating! Would this make a difference to the day? Do we tend to take things for granted until we are threatened with their loss?

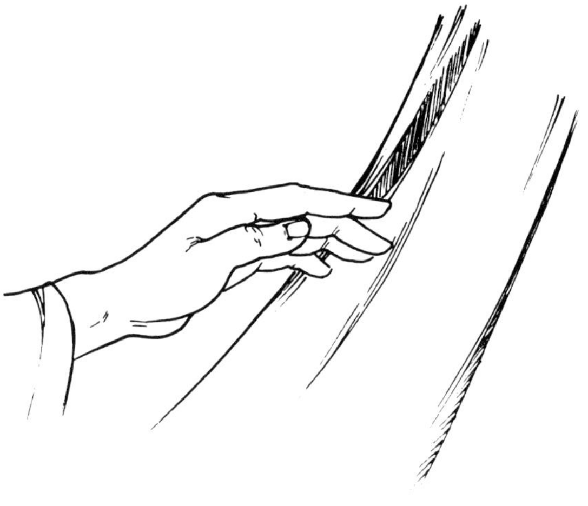

Reflection

Christians believe that Jesus' miracles were not performed just to impress or as tricks to show his power. They were always performed within a relationship, as part of a friendship. Are we sometimes more eager to impress people than to offer real help and friendship? Do we ever do the right thing for the wrong reason?

EIGHT

EVERYBODY WELCOME!

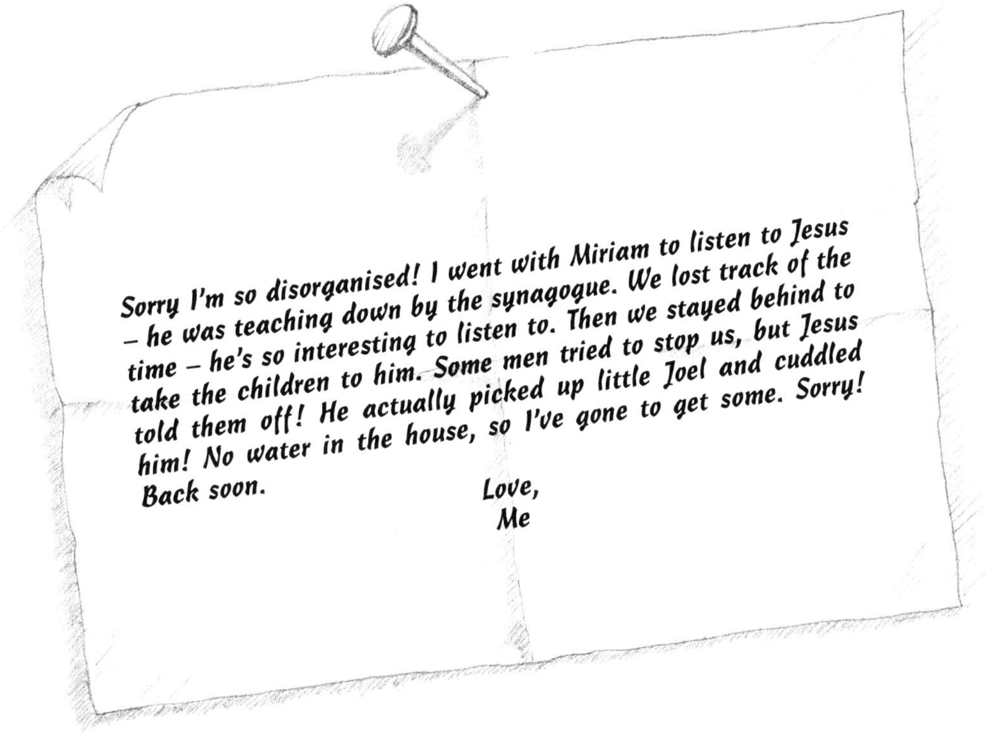

Sorry I'm so disorganised! I went with Miriam to listen to Jesus – he was teaching down by the synagogue. We lost track of the time – he's so interesting to listen to. Then we stayed behind to take the children to him. Some men tried to stop us, but Jesus told them off! He actually picked up little Joel and cuddled him! No water in the house, so I've gone to get some. Sorry! Back soon.
Love,
Me

Questions

1. Why had the crowd gone to Jesus?
2. What did the women want to do?
3. Why did the disciples try to stop them?

Activity

Think about the notices you see as you walk around school, shops, the town, and in cinemas. Some of them are just definite orders: 'No Parking'; 'Keep off the Grass'; 'Pay Here'; 'No Running in the Corridors'. But some notices are different: they have a different purpose: 'Everybody Welcome'; 'Please Come in'; 'Feel Free to Browse'.

If Jesus had held up a notice to the children, it would have read, 'Welcome everybody!' Can you design a notice for your classroom door that would welcome people who were visiting and the children in your class?

NOTE: We do not really know the names of any of the women and children who came to Jesus that day.

Everybody Welcome!

Jesus left Galilee and travelled towards Jerusalem. He knew that this was the last time he would travel this way before his death. In the villages, he often stopped to talk to the people and teach them, and to help and heal those who needed him. He had a lot of work to do, and he knew that time was short. Soon, he must be in Jerusalem for the Feast of the Passover.

The disciples knew that he was worried. They knew that he was in danger from his enemies, and they could see how busy he was. Everywhere he went, people asked for his help. There were always crowds waiting to hear him speak. He seldom had time alone, to rest. They listened now as he taught yet another crowd. When would he stop?

Then some women pushed through the other people. They were trying to bring their children to him. The disciples stepped forward hurriedly.

'No!' they told the women. 'He's tired, and busy teaching all these people. Don't disturb him. He won't want to stop just to see your children!'

The women were disappointed. They had all decided that they wanted Jesus to touch their children. The children were too young to understand or to remember what Jesus was saying, but Jesus was so powerful that surely a touch and a blessing from him would help their little ones throughout their lives! They turned away sadly to rejoin the crowd.

But Jesus had seen what had happened, and had heard his disciples. He understood that some people wanted him to bless their children, so that they could feel that their children too had met him. In any case, he had something important to teach everyone listening to him. He shouted over to the disciples: 'Don't stop them! Bring them to me. I want to see them.'

Quickly, the disciples gathered the women and children and took them over to Jesus. 'Remember this!' he told his listeners. 'Never stop children coming to me. You can all learn a lot from them. They are so trusting and eager to believe in people, and to please them. Anyone who wants to become a friend of God has to be like that.'

Then Jesus picked up each of the toddlers in turn. He took the babies from their mothers' arms, and cuddled them. He prayed that God would always look after these precious children. The mothers were overjoyed. They thanked him and hurried home to tell their friends and families about their day – to tell them how important children were to this great teacher, who had held their own boys and girls.

(This story can be found in Matthew 19:13–15; Mark 10:13–16; Luke 18:15–17.)

Background Information

Women: Women generally were held in low esteem in Jesus' day. Their interests were protected by certain laws, but they were not regarded as being men's equals in any sense. Jesus' treatment of and attitude to women is in direct contrast to this. He welcomed them into his group of followers and was happy for them to share in his teaching. He sometimes chose to teach in the Temple Court of the Women, rather than in the Men's Court, so that women could join him if they wished. Here, he welcomes the women, and recognises their wishes.

Children: Children, especially sons, were very important to the Jewish people at this time. However, people would still have been surprised at Jesus' welcome of these children, and at the suggestion that they themselves needed to become like the children in some ways. There are varying interpretations of Jesus' meaning in this passage. Different commentators highlight different qualities of children. I have tried to combine some of these in my interpretation of the meaning.

Conversation

A. Jesus said that his followers should be 'childlike', not 'childish'. Discuss the difference between the meanings of these two words.

B. At the time, women were not highly thought of. They were not fully valued as individuals, being known as the 'daughter' or 'mother' of somebody. Sons were valued far more highly than daughters. What does Jesus' behaviour here tell us about his attitude to women and to children?

C. We live in an age of hero-worship. It is common for personal belongings of our 'superstars' to be sold for large sums of money. People even preserve sweaty shirts or towels belonging to them!
What does the behaviour of the women tell you about Jesus' reputation at the time? Does this surprise you?

Reflection

Jesus always had time for those who needed him – even when he knew he was on the way to his death. Do we have time for people who need us? Or do we just pretend to be concerned.

Christians believe that Jesus still has time today for anyone who needs him.

NINE

WHO WILL HELP?

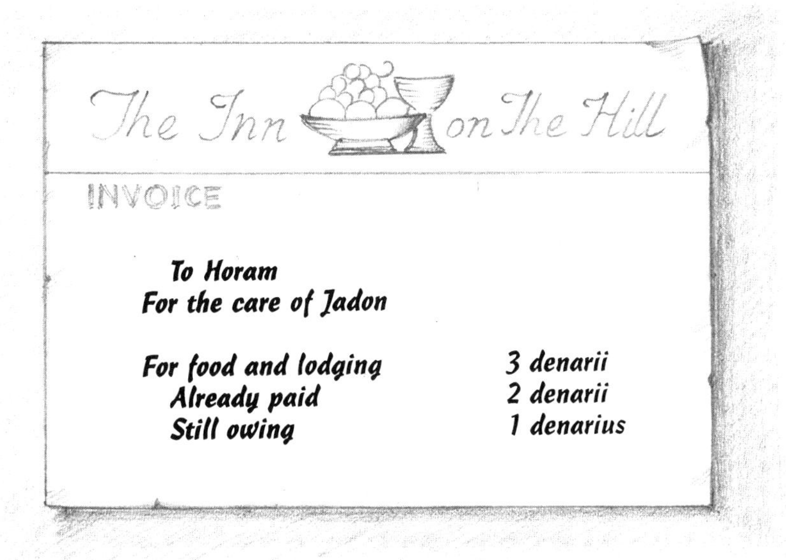

Questions

1. Why didn't the Priest and the Levite help the Traveller?

2. Were these real reasons for not helping him or made-up ones?

3. What did helping the Traveller cost the Samaritan as well as money?

Activity

Imagine you are the Traveller. Write about your journey. Your story could start:

I was very worried as I hurried along the road. I heard a noise – what was it?

If you prefer, you could write about the events as if you are the Priest or the Levite, explaining why you didn't help.

NOTE: We do not know what names, if any, Jesus gave to the Traveller and the Samaritan.

Who Will Help?

The man walked as quickly as he could up the steep, dusty road. His eyes searched the rocks on either side. He had never travelled alone along this road before, and now all the accounts he had heard about the robbers who worked here came back to him. Then he heard the sound he had been dreading: other footsteps in the stony, dry soil. He began to run, skidding, breathless – but he couldn't get away. The robbers had him.

Later, another traveller came hurrying along the road. He, too, was nervous. When he saw the man's bruised body lying at the side of the road, he glanced hurriedly round. He gathered up his long robes closely about his legs, crossed over to the other side of the road and rushed on. 'They might still be there, behind the rocks, waiting for me to stop!' he thought. 'And I have my job to think about. Anyway, he's probably dead already. I can't help him.'

And that's how it was with the next traveller. He was one of the religious leaders, too.

He saw the man – and hurried on. The man became weaker and weaker. The sun blazed down: he was desperately thirsty and in great pain.

At last, another traveller came. This one did not go straight past. He stopped, and knelt by the man. He bathed and bandaged his wounds. He helped him onto his donkey, and took him to the nearest inn. The man was astonished to learn that his rescuer was from Samaria.

'But why did you help me?' he asked. 'Surely all of you Samaritans hate us, just as we Jews hate you!'

The Samaritan shrugged his shoulders. 'You needed help,' he replied, 'and I was there. Rest now. I've paid for your keep. Stay until you feel strong enough to return home, and I'll pay anything extra next time I come.'

This is a story Jesus told to explain what God meant when he asked people to love their neighbour. He was saying, 'Your neighbour isn't just the person who lives next to you. It isn't just someone you know and like. It isn't even someone who lives in the same country as you, and who believes in the same things as you do – although it could be any of these. I mean that you should love and care for anyone who needs your help.'

The people listening to Jesus would have been surprised that the Samaritan helped the Jewish man, for the Samaritans and the Jews had been enemies for many years. Some Jews would walk for miles to avoid walking through Samaria. But Jesus loved the people of Samaria in the same way as he loved his own people the Jews. He

would travel through Samaria, stopping to talk to people there who needed his help.

The two people who did not help were a Priest and a Levite. These men worked in the Temple, the Jews' special place of worship in Jerusalem. If they touched or came near to a dead body, they would not have been able to do their work in the Temple for a while. So they were probably trying to avoid this. They were also afraid – quite naturally – that this was a trap.

The Samaritan helped the man, treating him as his neighbour, even though he was his enemy and despite his fears for his own safety.

(This story can be found in Luke 10:25–37.)

Background Information

Priests: The Priests were responsible for performing all the ritual duties in the Temple. They conducted the services of worship and prayer, and performed the sacrifices each day. They were also responsible for the teaching and interpretation of the Law.

Levites: The Levites worked as assistants to the Priests. They were responsible for organising and providing the music – both choral and instrumental – used in the Temple worship. Under Mosaic Law, both of these groups were rendered ritually impure by contact with a dead body. As such, they would have been unable to perform their Temple duties until a specified length of time had elapsed and certain rituals had been observed.

Samaria: There was a long-established enmity between the Jews and the Samaritans. A major factor in this was that the Jews regarded the Samaritans as being racially impure due to intermarriage with surrounding peoples. In retaliation, the Samaritans built their own Temple. The two peoples avoided each other whenever possible. Jesus travelled through Samaria, though, stopping to help a woman in need.

Road: This road snaked its way along an almost sheer, rock-strewn valley side. It was well-known as a place of ambush by robbers. Ironically, it was used by some Galileans, in spite of its dangers, to avoid travelling through Samaria.

Inn: The Romans set up an efficient system of inns through their Empire. But this is more likely to be a small local inn, probably little more than a home open for travellers in need. We have little idea of the charges made by such places.

Denarius: A denarius was a Roman coin. We know from Matthew 20:1–16 that it was roughly a day's wages for a casual agricultural labourer.

Oil and Wine: The Samaritan used olive oil and wine on the Traveller's wounds. Oil was often used to soothe wounds, and the wine may have been used for cleansing.

Conversation

A. Imagine you were one of the people listening to Jesus as he told this story. You have been taught to dislike and mistrust the Samaritans! How would you feel as you listened to this story?

B. If you were a Samaritan listening to Jesus, how would you feel hearing a Jewish teacher telling this story?

C. Does this story teach us anything today?

Reflection

The Priest and the Levite saw the Traveller as a problem to be avoided. The Samaritan saw a person in need, even though he was an enemy. Do you sometimes think of people as problems instead of being people just like you?

TEN

THE FATHER WHO WAITED

Questions

1. Why did Simon leave home?

2. How do you think the father felt when his son left?

3. What do we learn about Simon's friends in this story?

NOTE: This is a story told by Jesus to help people understand what God is like. We do not know if Jesus gave the son a name, but we will call him Simon.

Activity

The father was waiting for his son to come home. If he had known where he was, he might have sent him a letter. Imagine you are the father. What do you think he would have written?

The Father Who Waited

The young man, Simon, sat on a rock, huddled up in his tattered cloak. He watched the scrawny pigs in front of him as they snorted and rooted in the dust for the food he had just scattered there. 'I'm so hungry, I could almost eat that stuff,' he thought. Closing his eyes, he thought back to how life had been for him on his father's farm, just a few short months ago.

He had had everything he needed then, living with his father and brother. 'And I gave it all up,' he thought bitterly, 'just because I wanted to see the world instead of working on the farm. And look where I've ended up – starving on someone else's farm!'

'Give me my share of the money!' he had told his father. 'I shall have it when you're dead. Let me have it now while I can enjoy it.' Sadly, his father had given it to him, and watched him leave.

Now, Simon thought back to his wonderful new life, far from home. He thought about the extravagant clothes he wore, and the great parties he had given. 'I had plenty of friends then,' he realised, 'when I had money to spend. But they soon abandoned me when it ran out!' Unable to pay his bills, he had ended up feeding pigs. 'Even my father's servants live better than I do now!' he thought.

Suddenly, he stood up. 'I'm going home!' he said aloud. 'I'll admit I was wrong and ask Dad to forgive me. I wouldn't blame him if he refuses: but at least he might take me on as a servant on the farm.'

So he set off. He didn't expect a welcome: he just wanted to be forgiven and to live in some comfort again. It was a long, hard walk, but at last he could see familiar countryside. He was very tired. As he stopped to rest, he noticed dust rising on the track ahead. Who was coming? He shaded his eyes. 'It looks like Dad,' he said, 'but it can't be!' In a few minutes, he knew for sure that it was! Was his father so angry with him that he didn't even want him on his land? He waited anxiously – and his father ran up to him, and threw his arms around him!

'At last!' he cried. 'I've waited so long for you – every day since you went, up on that hill so that I would see you as soon as you came. Come on, let's go home, son.'

But Simon pushed him away. 'No, Dad. I don't deserve to come home as your son. I know that what I did was wrong. I'm very sorry. Let me live at the farm as your servant. That's all I ask.'

But his father disagreed! 'No! You come home as my son. You shall have everything you need. And I shall give you a ring to wear, so that everyone will know that I still want you as my son. Come home!'

This is a parable, a story told by Jesus to help his listeners understand his teaching. In this case, he wanted them to learn more about God and his love for them.

(This story can be found in Luke 15:11–32.)

Background Information

Inheritance: The son is correct when he says that some of the money will be his on the death of his father. Inheritance was to the sons of family first, with the eldest son receiving a double share. A daughter inherited if there were no sons, and then the wealth passed to the nearest male relative.

Pigs: Pigs were ritually unclean animals to the Jewish people. They were forbidden to eat their flesh, and even touching one rendered a Jew ritually unclean. It is a mark of the son's desperation and degradation that he is reduced to looking after pigs. These animals were probably owned by a settler in the land. Greeks, for instance, settled in an area near Lake Galilee, and they did eat pork.

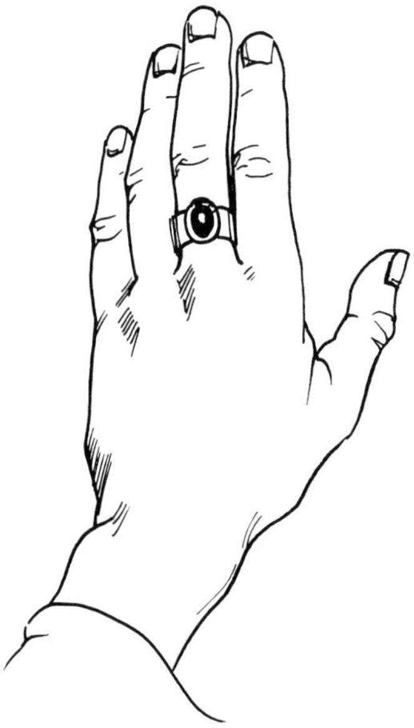

Ring: The father makes it obvious that the boy is returning as his son, into the full rights and privileges this entails. The ring was a symbol of this. Christians believe that they, too, are accepted into God's family as 'sons,' with all the rights this entails.

Shepherds: The shepherd's job referred to in this section was very different from the job of a shepherd in this country. He would lead his flock of sheep (and, possibly, goats) from place to place seeking fresh, gently running water and good grazing. This would entail travelling considerable distances. There would be continual danger from wild animals. The shepherds we watch working the sheep on the hills drive their animals, with the help of dogs: Biblical shepherds led their animals.

Conversation

A. Christians believe that Jesus told this story to teach people about God. If God is like the father in the story, what does this tell Christians about him?

B. What exactly did the son do wrong? He didn't steal the money, after all. Did he steal anything?

C. The son's new friends in the city were very different from his father. Can you point out the differences between them?

Reflection

Living in a family or in any group brings responsibilities to us as well as advantages and privileges. We owe certain things to others, as well as being owed things by them. Do we sometimes find it easier to claim our rights than to live up to our responsibilities?

ELEVEN

'AND NOW SAY THANK YOU!'

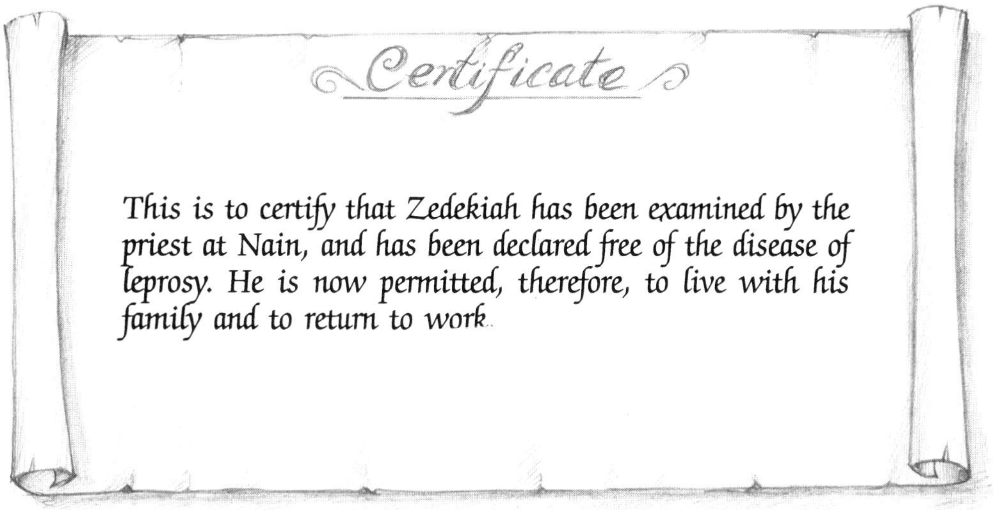

Certificate
This is to certify that Zedekiah has been examined by the priest at Nain, and has been declared free of the disease of leprosy. He is now permitted, therefore, to live with his family and to return to work.

Questions

1. Why were the men not living at home?

2. How did the people treat them?

3. How does the story say that Jesus helped them?

Activity

Their families must have been very glad to see the men again! Write a letter as if it is from one of their children telling a friend what had happened to his/her family.

NOTE: We do not know the real names of any of the lepers in this story. I have called the man from Samaria Zedekiah.

The children might wish to send for some information about leprosy and its treatment today from a charity involved in this work. Lepra's address is Fairfax House, Causton Road, Colchester, Essex, CO1 1PU. An S.A.E. would be appreciated.

'And Now Say Thank You!'

The man drew his tattered cloak more closely round his knees as he sat hunched up at the side of the dusty track. Around him sat his nine companions – other men like him who had been forced to leave their homes and loving families, and become beggars, living outside the towns and villages. He was not a Jew like them: he was from Samaria, for this was the border between Galilee and Samaria. But in their struggle to live, the old hatred was forgotten. A traveller walked by, making sure that he stayed well away from the pitiful group of men. He threw a loaf of bread to them. They shared it round as they shouted, 'Thank you,' to him – but he had already hurried on. He didn't want to catch what they'd got! He was staying well away!

For these ten men had leprosy, a skin disease that people then thought was easy to catch. As soon as their skin showed the first signs of the disease, the men had to leave their homes. They were ordered to stay well away from everyone else. Groups of men and women like them lived all over the country, in caves or rough shelters, thinking all the time of their own homes and longing to see their families again.

The man had finished his small share of the bread. He was hungry! He understood how frightened other people were of him. He had been the same! Some of them were as kind as they could be, leaving them the food they could spare, or even old clothes. But it was a terrible life. He sighed as he looked down the track. What he saw there made him struggle to his feet. 'Look!' he shouted. 'A crowd is coming. Look at all that dust. Perhaps some of them will buy us some food!'

They waited eagerly. Why were so many people coming to this small village? When the first people reached them, they asked, 'What is it? Where are you all going?'

'It's Jesus – Jesus of Nazareth!' they were told. 'He's on his way up to Jerusalem.'

The men looked at each other. Jesus! They had heard about him as they listened to travellers passing by. They knew about all the people he had helped and healed. 'Do you think he could help us?' they whispered to each other. 'If only he could!'

It was easy to see which man was Jesus. The crowd jostled round him, trying to hear everything he said. The men dared not go any nearer: people sometimes threw stones to keep them away! They shouted, 'Jesus, Lord, please help us!'

Jesus stopped and looked at them. He saw the desperation in their faces, and knew how they suffered. And he saw that they really believed that he was able to help them. 'Go to the priest in the village,' he told them. 'Ask him to examine you.'

The men looked at each other – and then set off as quickly as they could. And on the way, they realised that something incredible had happened. Their skin was whole again! All signs of the disease had gone! 'We are healed!' they shouted. 'We can go home again!' And nine of them hurried on to the priest.

But one man turned round. He wanted to go home too, but he had something to do first. He hurried back to Jesus. This time he went right up to him, and knelt at his feet. 'Thank you Jesus,' he said. 'Thank you for healing me!'

'Where are the others?' Jesus asked, looking round. 'Weren't they cured too?' He turned to the crowd. 'Only this man has come to say thank you – even though he is not from our country.'

'You are healed because you believed in me and in my power to heal you,' he told the man. 'Go to the priest now, and then return to your normal life.'

(This story can be found in Luke 17:11–19.)

Background Information

Leprosy: Part of the duties of Priests in biblical times was to enforce the Laws. These not only covered areas of religious life, but also the area we would now call public health. Some of these related to infectious diseases. It is possible that several skin diseases were classed together as 'leprosy', including the group we now recognise as leprosy. It was then thought that leprosy was highly contagious, and anyone adjudged by the Priests to be suffering from it had to leave his family, and live away from human habitation, relying on the charity of passers-by to leave food for them. Colonies of lepers were common outside towns. They had to stay away from people, and warn others of their presence by shouting, 'Unclean!' if anyone approached. The Priests had a duty to examine them regularly in case the disease disappeared. A person could not return to his family unless a Priest pronounced him cured, and he then took part in elaborate purification ceremonies. Nowadays, we know that leprosy is not highly contagious, but isolation still occurs in some countries. We do not know how the Priest made known the fact that someone could return home: I have imagined that a certificate was issued.

Miracles: The miracles of Jesus were not performed just to gain attention and followers through sensation. In fact, he often asked people not to tell others about them. They always occur within a relationship: there is always faith present, either in the person helped or in the people bringing them to Jesus. Jesus stressed healing of the whole person: they need a right relationship with God. The miracles were to be signs, also, of Jesus' true identity. They made people think about who he was.

Conversation

A. People still suffer from leprosy today, but now we know much more about it. We know that it is not easy for people to catch leprosy from someone living with them, and we can now treat it successfully with drugs. Why did these men have to live like this?

B. The people with leprosy suffered because of other people's ignorance and prejudice. What do these words mean? Do any people suffer today because of the same things?

C. How important is it for us to say thank you and to be grateful to other people? What does Jesus' reaction tell us? The Bible says that the other men were all healed, and stayed healed, even though they did not say thank you!

Reflection

Prejudice means pre-judging someone before we know the truth about them. When you meet someone, do you make up your own mind about them, after getting to know them for yourself, or do you decide to agree with your friends?

TWELVE

'BUT HE DOESN'T DESERVE IT!'

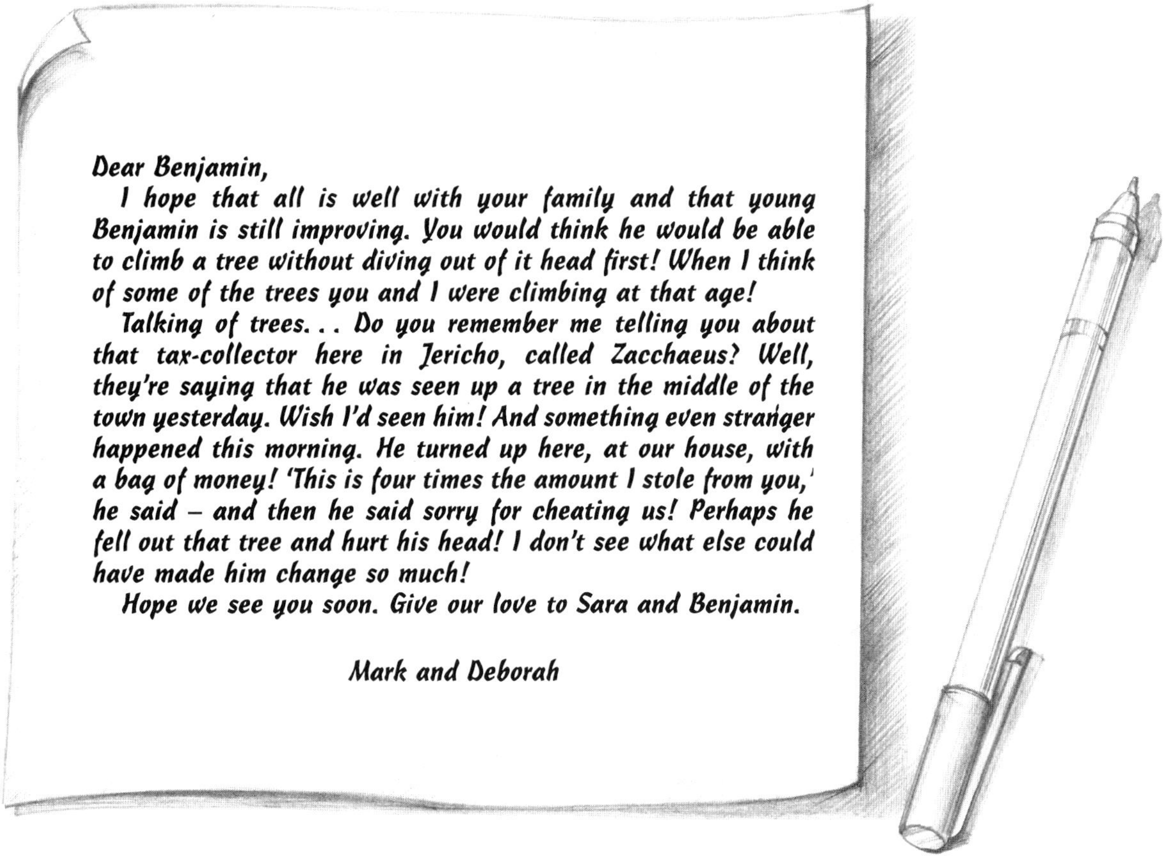

Dear Benjamin,

I hope that all is well with your family and that young Benjamin is still improving. You would think he would be able to climb a tree without diving out of it head first! When I think of some of the trees you and I were climbing at that age!

Talking of trees... Do you remember me telling you about that tax-collector here in Jericho, called Zacchaeus? Well, they're saying that he was seen up a tree in the middle of the town yesterday. Wish I'd seen him! And something even stranger happened this morning. He turned up here, at our house, with a bag of money! 'This is four times the amount I stole from you,' he said – and then he said sorry for cheating us! Perhaps he fell out that tree and hurt his head! I don't see what else could have made him change so much!

Hope we see you soon. Give our love to Sara and Benjamin.

Mark and Deborah

Questions

1. How did the crowd feel about Zacchaeus? How did they show this by their treatment of him?

2. What had Zacchaeus done to deserve this treatment?

3. How did Jesus treat Zacchaeus? Can you suggest why he treated him like this?

Activity

In his letter, Mark says that he has already told Benjamin about Zacchaeus. Write the letter in which he told Benjamin about the tax-collector.

REMEMBER! Mark is a made-up character. Zacchaeus and Jesus are in the Bible story.

'But He Doesn't Deserve It!'

Zacchaeus was a tax-collector for the Romans in Jericho. Nobody liked him very much. He always collected more tax than the Romans wanted, and kept the extra for himself. He became richer and richer, and more and more hated! It was bad enough to work for the Romans in the first place, but to use them as an excuse to cheat his own people was even worse.

One day, Jesus travelled through Jericho on his way to Jerusalem. Zacchaeus joined the crowds thronging the streets. Like them, he wanted to see this man for himself. Zacchaeus could hear people talking about the many wonderful things Jesus had done.

'They say he healed ten people of leprosy,' one said.

'Yes,' added another eagerly, 'and he's just healed Bartimaeus here in Jericho! Bartimaeus can see perfectly now, after all these years.'

'He's coming!' shouted a man at the front of the crowd. 'Jesus is here!'

Zacchaeus could not see! He tried to push his way through, but, as soon as the people saw who he was, they refused to let him through.

'I must see him,' Zacchaeus thought. He looked round for help – and spotted a tree, its branches overhanging the street. He hurried over to it. He hadn't climbed a tree for years – but somehow he managed to squirm up the sturdy trunk and out along a branch. He didn't want anyone to see him: how they would laugh at him if they did!

From his branch, he could see Jesus clearly as he slowly made his way through the crowds. He was very near now, almost under Zacchaeus' tree. Was this man really able to do those wonderful things?

Suddenly, Jesus stopped. He looked straight up into the tree – and said, 'Zacchaeus, come down now. Hurry up! I'm on my way to your house.'

Zacchaeus was amazed! As he scrambled down, he asked himself, 'How does he know my name? How did he know I was there? Does he know what I'm like?'

The crowd was amazed too. 'He can't know who Zacchaeus is – or what he's like,' someone muttered. 'How can he want anything to do with him?' But Jesus did know about Zacchaeus. He knew everything about him. Zacchaeus walked home with Jesus, feeling surprised and pleased that Jesus wanted to be with him.

As he listened to Jesus during the meal, he realised that Jesus cared about him – Zacchaeus the hated tax-collector! He learned how wrong he had been to cheat people, and saw that he could put things right! 'I'll give half my money to people who need it,' he told Jesus, 'and I'll repay four times over any money I stole. I want to show how sorry I am.' And Zacchaeus realised that, although he had loved him just as he was, Jesus was now very pleased with him, too.

There were a lot of very surprised people in Jericho during the next few days. But Zacchaeus was the most surprised and the happiest! His whole life had changed. He had met Jesus.

(This story can be found in Luke 19:1–10.)

Background Information

The Romans had invaded and defeated Palestine some years before Jesus was born. They encouraged some of the Jews to collect the taxes they imposed on the people, to save themselves trouble, and to try to redirect some of the hostility the conquered people felt. These agents of the Romans were unpopular as they were seen as traitors to their own race. Also, many of them seized this opportunity of making money for themselves by collecting sums over and above the rates demanded by the Romans. They were held in such low esteem that they were not even allowed to give evidence in Jewish courts, or to hold religious or public office. Jesus' enemies often expressed surprise when he associated with tax-collectors (publicans). In fact one of his twelve disciples was a tax-collector – Levi, later known as Matthew. Jesus' reply was that he had come to help anybody who needed him.

Zacchaeus was a chief tax-collector, responsible for a whole district. Zacchaeus gave back more money than the law demanded when he paid four times the amount stolen. There were various rules, but a usual figure was reached by adding a further one fifth to the amount.

The biblical account adds that Zacchaeus could not see over the crowd because he was short.

Conversation

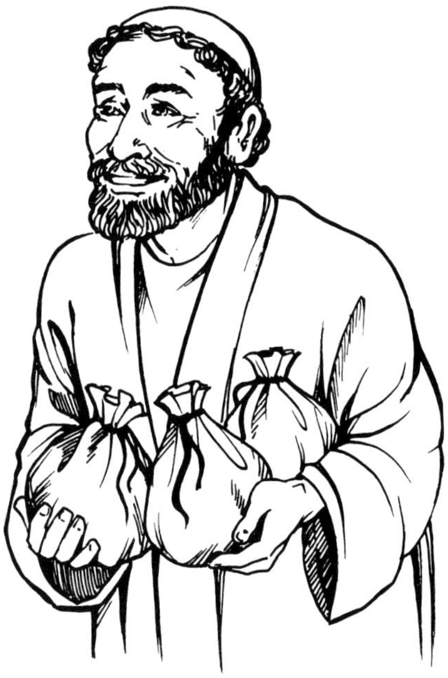

1. Zacchaeus was used to rejection. How do you think he felt when Jesus stopped and spoke to him kindly? What does this tell people about the character of Jesus?

2. Zacchaeus changed on the inside. How did he show this to other people? Is it enough just to be sorry when we have hurt other people?

3. Jesus was on his way to Jerusalem for the last time when he passed through Jericho. He knew he was going to die there. But he stopped to help a blind man called Bartimaeus and Zacchaeus. What does this tell people about Jesus?

Reflection

If you had been Mark or Deborah, would you have believed in Zacchaeus' change of heart? What would have convinced you?

THIRTEEN

DEAD!

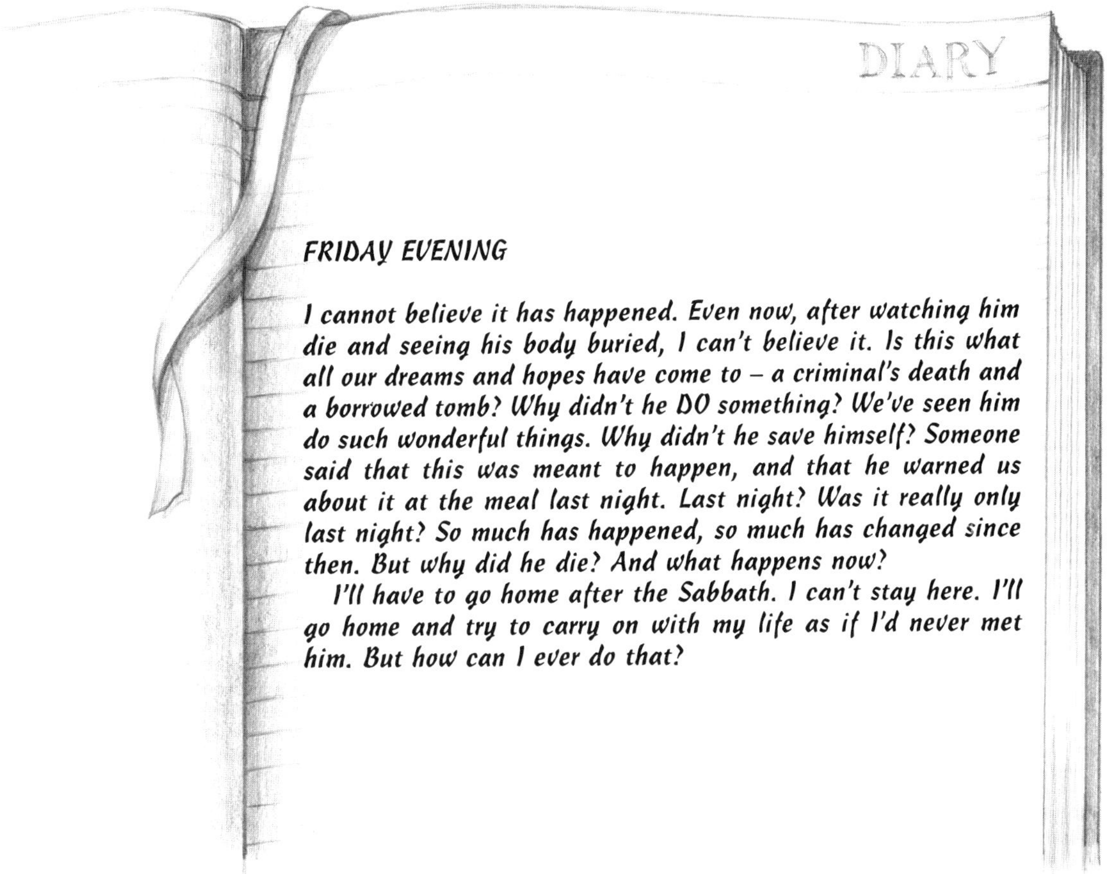

DIARY
FRIDAY EVENING
I cannot believe it has happened. Even now, after watching him die and seeing his body buried, I can't believe it. Is this what all our dreams and hopes have come to – a criminal's death and a borrowed tomb? Why didn't he DO something? We've seen him do such wonderful things. Why didn't he save himself? Someone said that this was meant to happen, and that he warned us about it at the meal last night. Last night? Was it really only last night? So much has happened, so much has changed since then. But why did he die? And what happens now?
I'll have to go home after the Sabbath. I can't stay here. I'll go home and try to carry on with my life as if I'd never met him. But how can I ever do that?

Questions

1. Why was Peter still upset when they reached the garden?

2. Why didn't Jesus go to sleep as the disciples did?

3. Who did Jesus ask to look after his mother?

Activity

We do not really know what Thaddaeus was doing or thinking during Jesus' arrest and death. But we do know more about Peter. Write Peter's diary entry for this time, describing what he did and thought.

NOTE: Thaddaeus was one of Jesus' special followers, the disciples. We do not know very much about him.

Dead!

It was dark and quiet in the garden. Jesus often came to places like this to talk with God. And now he had something very important to ask him. He walked off quietly by himself.

After Jesus had left them, the disciples sat and talked softly about the meal they had just shared with him. Peter was still upset. 'He said I would let him down and lie about him. I would never do that!' he told James indignantly. And what about Judas, Peter wondered, who still hadn't come back after leaving when Jesus had said that one of them would betray him to his enemies. Where was he now?

But they were tired and it was late. Soon, they rolled themselves in their cloaks and fell asleep.

Jesus was not sleeping. In another part of the garden, he was talking to God his Father. He knew that pain and death lay ahead for him: they were very close now. 'Is this the only thing I can do to help men and women become friends with you, Father? If there is any other way, then please don't let me suffer the things that are coming,' he prayed. 'But if this is the only way, then, however terrible it is for me, I will do it. I only want to do what you want me to do.' So he prayed, asking that God would help him in the lonely hours ahead.

Suddenly the peace of the garden was shattered. Armed guards, led by Judas, rushed to Jesus and seized him, dragging him off for trial. The disciples, terrified and confused, forgot their promises to stay with Jesus and fled. Peter followed secretly, and waited outside the high priest's house where Jesus was being tried.

There he was recognised as being one of Jesus' disciples. Frightened for his life, Peter denied it. 'I don't even know the man!' he yelled – and immediately realised that he had done just what Jesus had said he would do. He was heartbroken: how could he have let down his friend so badly?

Hours later, Jesus was fastened to the cross and left to die. As he grew weaker, he thought of the people around him. He asked John, one of his disciples, to look after his mother Mary. He begged God to forgive the people who were killing him. As his death drew near, he suffered great pain. But as he died, he shouted in triumph, 'It is complete! I have done it!'

Then he died. He had finished what God had asked him to do.

Nicodemus and Joseph of Arimathea had been secret followers of Jesus. Now, in their grief, they forgot their fear. They took his body and laid it in a borrowed tomb rolling a great rock over the entrance to close it. The leaders were afraid that his disciples might take the body, to pretend he was still alive. They placed a guard on the tomb. And the disciples, confused, miserable and frightened, went into hiding.

(This story can be found in Luke 22:7–62 and 23:34 and John 19:16–42.)

Background Information

Crucifixion was the usual Roman method of execution, especially for rebellion. A Roman writer acknowledged that it was a very cruel death. The Jews' usual method was death by stoning: under Roman law, they were forbidden to carry out the death penalty, so they were forced to bring Jesus before Pilate the Roman Governor in order to receive the death penalty. Pilate would have been in Jerusalem with his troops, as it was the Passover, to ensure public order. Jerusalem would be crowded with people who had come to celebrate the festival there.

Herod would have been in Jerusalem, his capital and location of the Temple, for the Passover Feast. As nominal King under the Romans, he had a duty to try Jesus.

Burial: Burial on the same day as death was common. In this case, the Jewish authorities were keen to ensure burial before the Sabbath began at sunset on Friday evening. For those who could afford them, the usual place of burial was in caves, either natural or man-made. The body would be sprinkled with spices and wrapped in a shroud, with a cloth placed over the face, before being laid on a slab hewn out of the cave wall. Jesus was laid in a tomb that had been made for Joseph of Arimathea: Joseph had been a secret follower of Jesus, for fear of his fellow rulers.

Jewish leaders: Care must be taken to avoid giving the impression that all the Jews opposed Jesus. He was a Jew, as were his disciples and supporters. His enemies disliked him for several reasons: racial prejudice was not one of them.

NOTE: There are big questions involved in the Crucifixion which are not dealt with in this section. Please see the section on such issues in the Introduction.

Conversation

A. What were the disciples doing while Jesus was praying in the garden? How do you think he felt about them doing this while he was so upset?

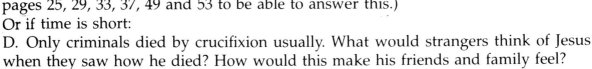

B. While Jesus was dying, he said three things. Read them carefully. What do they tell people about the sort of person Jesus was?

C. Only criminals died by crucifixion usually. Had Jesus done anything to deserve such a death? (Children will need to have read the sections on pages 25, 29, 33, 37, 49 and 53 to be able to answer this.)

Or if time is short:

D. Only criminals died by crucifixion usually. What would strangers think of Jesus when they saw how he died? How would this make his friends and family feel?

Reflection

On the cross, Jesus asked God to forgive the people who were killing him. Christians believe that God will forgive anyone who is sorry for what they have done and wants to change. Think about how easy or difficult you find it to forgive other people.

FOURTEEN

ALIVE!

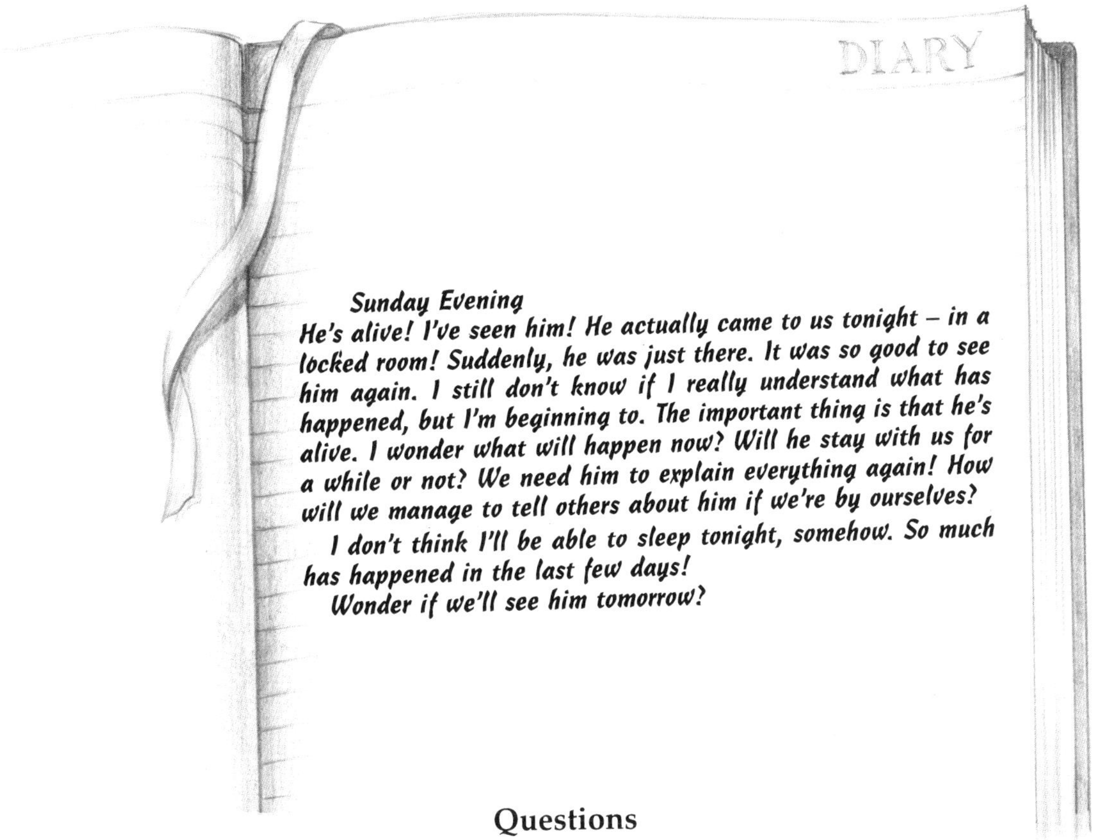

DIARY
Sunday Evening
He's alive! I've seen him! He actually came to us tonight – in a locked room! Suddenly, he was just there. It was so good to see him again. I still don't know if I really understand what has happened, but I'm beginning to. The important thing is that he's alive. I wonder what will happen now? Will he stay with us for a while or not? We need him to explain everything again! How will we manage to tell others about him if we're by ourselves?
I don't think I'll be able to sleep tonight, somehow. So much has happened in the last few days!
Wonder if we'll see him tomorrow?

Questions

1. Why had Mary Magdalene gone to the tomb?

2. Why were the disciples in hiding?

3. Can you make a list of the people Jesus came to after he had risen?

Activity

The Bible does not tell us how Thaddaeus felt when he knew Jesus was alive again. But it does tell us about Thomas, another disciple. He was not with the others in the room when Jesus came, and he found he could not believe that he was really alive. He said, 'Unless I see and touch the nail-marks, I will not believe he is alive!' (John 20:25 paraphrased). So Jesus returned a week later to the same room, when Thomas was there. He showed Thomas his wounds, and let him touch them; and Thomas believed. 'My Lord and my God,' he said. Write a diary entry for Thomas. It could be for a day in that week while he was the only disciple who did not know that Jesus was alive. Or it could be one written after he had seen Jesus.

NOTE: Thaddaeus was one of the disciples. The Bible does not tell us much about him. I have imagined that he kept a diary.

Alive!

It was very quiet in the garden after Peter and John had left. Mary Magdalene watched them go. What were they thinking, she wondered. They had come with her as soon as she gave them the angel's message. Did they believe him? John had seemed happier when he left, she thought. She turned away from the empty tomb. She still held the fragrant spices she had brought to anoint Jesus' body. It wasn't much to do for him, but it was all she could do now that he was dead. But even that was now impossible, for his body had disappeared.

She sighed, and wiped her eyes with the edge of her robe. What had the messenger, the angel, said when he sent her to fetch the disciples – that Jesus was alive? How could that be? She had watched him die. Even now, his enemies were not satisfied. They had hidden his body.

She became aware that someone was walking along the path behind her. She turned round, trying to see who it was through her tears. If it was the gardener, he might know where the body was.

'Why are you crying?' he asked.

'Please, sir, if you know where Jesus' body is, please tell me.'

But the man simply said, 'Mary.' And it was Jesus' voice. He was alive!

'Teacher!' she cried, and she would have grasped his hand but he stopped her.

'No, I am not staying here now,' he told her. 'Tell my disciples that I will see them in Jerusalem,' and he left her there in the quiet garden.

That evening, the disciples again met in a locked room. They still expected Jesus' enemies to arrest them, too, at any moment. They were very confused. They didn't understand how Jesus could be alive – and yet here was Peter, insisting that Jesus had come to him, and Mary Magdalene said that she had met Jesus at the empty tomb. They argued over and over. Just what had Jesus said about his death and about what would happen next? If only they could be sure!

A knock on the door! Who was it? Relieved, they recognised Cleopas' voice, and let him and his friend in, carefully relocking the door after them. What were they doing back in Jerusalem? They had only just left! In amazement, they heard how a man had joined them on their journey home. He had explained to them why Jesus had died. Then, at Cleopas' home, they had suddenly realised that the man was Jesus himself! They had hurried back to tell the others.

Before the disciples could take this in, Jesus himself was there with them! They fell silent. Some of them were frightened. Who or what – was this who had come through locked doors, looking like their dead teacher?

Jesus smiled. 'Don't worry!' he told them. 'It is really me! Feel me – I'm as solid as you are. Have you anything to eat in here?'

And, as he ate, they gradually accepted that Jesus was alive. Then he explained to them why he had died.

Jesus came to his disciples many more times.

He met them on the beach one day and cooked them a barbecued fish breakfast! Once, he came to a crowd of hundreds. Many people saw him! But soon the time came for him to leave the earth and to return to his Father. 'I will send the Holy Spirit to you, as I promised,' he told the disciples. 'Stay in Jerusalem until he comes. He will be with you always, helping you as you tell others about me and about my love for them.' And then he left them, and returned to his Father.

(This story can be found in all the Gospels. This account is selected from: Matthew 28:1–10; Mark 16:1–18; Luke 24:1–49; John 20:1–21: 25.)

Background Information

Resurrection: By New Testament times, most people in Judea believed in resurrection; but the Sadducees did not. Christians believe in resurrection. The gospel writers go to some trouble to point out that Jesus was not a 'ghost' or a revived corpse. He had a new 'body', different in some ways from his former one. He ate in front of witnesses, and encouraged Thomas to touch him. The disciples certainly were in no doubt that he had risen. Their lives and their behaviour were transformed. Jesus' resurrection is a central tenet of Christians' faith. It shows them that death and wrong have been defeated. It is Jesus' victory over all the negative, wrong things in life. Jesus took everything that evil could throw at him, and still came out living and loving. This is why Easter Sunday is such a celebration for Christians. It is the day when they remember especially the resurrection, and celebrate that Jesus is still alive to be their friend.

Enemies of Jesus: Not all of the Jewish religious leaders opposed Jesus. Jesus himself and his followers were Jews.

Conversation

A. Why did the disciples find it so difficult to believe that Jesus was alive? How did he convince them?

B. Women were not highly thought of at the time! It was unusual for men to allow women to follow them and to listen to their teaching. Mary Magdalene had been healed by Jesus. And yet it is she – a woman – who sees Jesus first. What does this tell you about Jesus?

C. Christians believe that Jesus' rising from death showed that he had defeated wrong and death. Why do you think this belief is important to them today?

Reflection

Springtime is a time of new life and new beginnings. It is the natural time for many animals and birds to be born or hatched, and it is good to see the spring flowers, and new leaves on the trees after the winter. For Christians, Easter is a special time of new birth, a new beginning. For to them Jesus' resurrection is a reminder that their new life has begun as Jesus' followers.

FIFTEEN

WHAT A CHANGE!

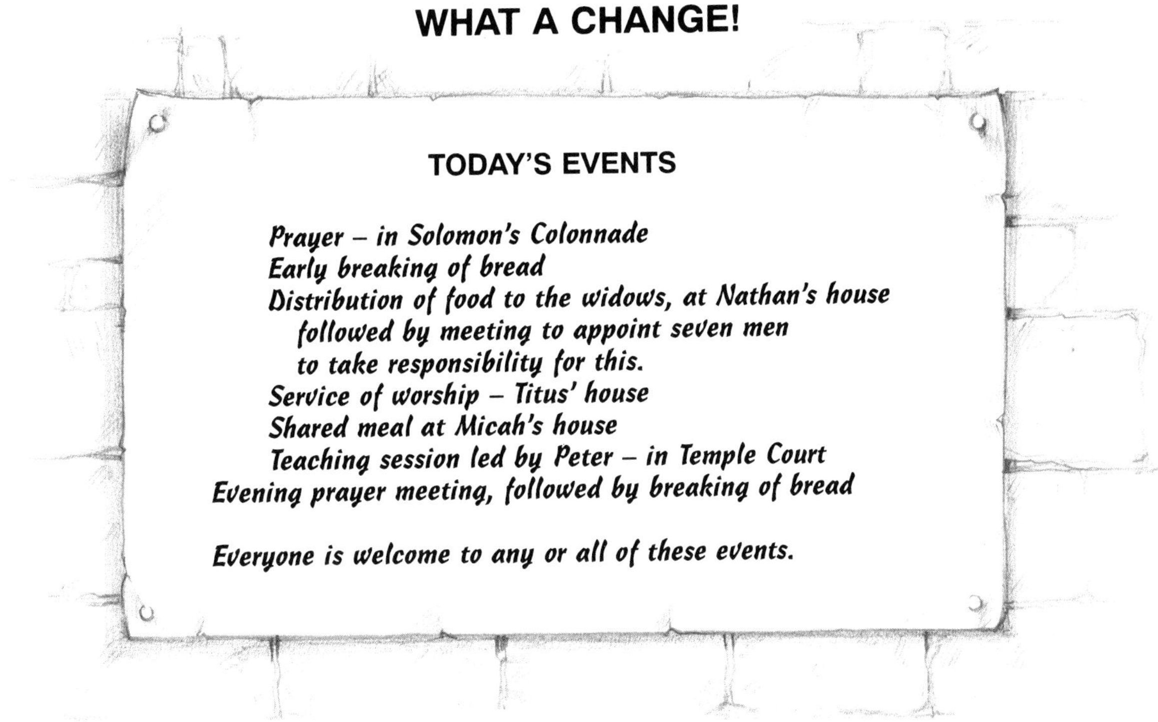

TODAY'S EVENTS
Prayer – in Solomon's Colonnade
Early breaking of bread
Distribution of food to the widows, at Nathan's house followed by meeting to appoint seven men to take responsibility for this.
Service of worship – Titus' house
Shared meal at Micah's house
Teaching session led by Peter – in Temple Court
Evening prayer meeting, followed by breaking of bread
Everyone is welcome to any or all of these events.

Questions

1. Why did the disciples stay in Jerusalem? What were they waiting for?

2. How did the disciples know that something special was happening when the Holy Spirit came to them?

3. Can you list three things that the early believers did together?

Activity

Different word-pictures are used to help us to understand what the Holy Spirit is like: at Jesus' baptism, he is described as a dove; at Pentecost, he is described as a wind and as fire. Choose one of these symbols. Choose a way of representing it in artwork that you think would be appropriate to the symbol. You could use paint, printing, wax-resist pictures, or collage, for instance.

(Conversation C could be done first if wished.)

NOTE: Micah, Titus, and Nathan are made up names for some of the early believers.

What A Change!

'Stay in Jerusalem,' Jesus had said to the disciples. 'Soon I will send the Holy Spirit to you.'

So each day the disciples met together to pray and to praise God. They discussed everything they could remember about the Holy Spirit, the Helper whom Jesus was going to send to them. They remembered that Jesus had told them that the Holy Spirit would be a Helper who would stay with them forever. He would remind them of Jesus' teaching, and would help them when they were in difficult situations. He would comfort them when they were unhappy, and he would bring them power to do God's work well.

And, early one morning, as they talked about these things, the Holy Spirit came! There was a great roaring, as if a strong wind was rushing through the room. As they looked at each other in astonishment, they saw what looked like fire descending over them. It seemed as if flames left the fire, one hovering over the head of each of them. And they knew immediately that the Holy Spirit was there with them, inside them. They were filled with joy! They were no longer alone! They began to thank God for this great gift and to praise him – and they discovered that they were speaking in languages they had never learned! Soon, all of them were singing and shouting their own songs of praise to God!

Of course, other people – in the streets and houses around – heard them. There were always many Jews from other lands visiting Jerusalem to see the Temple and to worship God there. These people each heard their own language being shouted! They were amazed. 'These men are only ordinary men from Galilee,' they said. 'How can they know so many languages?'

But other people did not think it was puzzling at all! 'They're drunk!' they retorted. 'They're speaking nonsense!'

So Peter spoke to the crowd. He explained to them that Jesus was the Messiah for whom they had waited so long. He told them how they, too, could become friends of God, like the disciples themselves. And he explained what had happened that day. So many of them believed what he said that about three thousand people joined the disciples there and then!

Then there began a busy time for them all. Each day they met together to pray and to worship God. They shared a simple meal together, just as Jesus had told them to at the Last Supper. The disciples shared all they knew about Jesus with the new believers, and the Holy Spirit gave them the power to heal people. One of these was a lame man who for years had begged at a gate of the Temple. Peter healed him and when the crowd saw this man jumping and running, they realised something amazing had happened. Peter was able to tell them, too, the truth about Jesus.

None of the believers was needy or hungry, for they all shared things together. They took special care of the widows among them, who had no husband to earn money. After much prayer, they chose seven people to look after these women, to ensure they were given what they needed.

One of these men was Stephen. Some of the leaders did not like him, and they plotted against him. Some people believed that Jesus was a fake, an imposter. These people wanted to stop others believing in him. They had Stephen killed, just because he believed in Jesus. Then they began to persecute the other Christians too. Many Christians were imprisoned and cruelly treated. So some of the others left Jerusalem: and everywhere they went, they told people about Jesus. And more and more people came to believe in him. Their enemies could not silence them.

(This story can be found in Acts 2:1–8:1.)

Background Information

Disciples: This is the name given to the twelve men chosen by Jesus to be his special followers who would spread the message about him after he had returned to his Father. It means 'learners'.

Apostles: This word means 'those who are sent', or 'messengers'. The disciples became known as the apostles after Jesus 'sent them into all the world' to teach about him, after the Ascension when Jesus returned to his Father.

The Holy Spirit: Christians believe that the Holy Spirit is part of the Trinity of God along with God the Father and Jesus the Son. They believe he is God present and active now, a real but invisible friend, helping them to live as Christians. The children should not be allowed to feel any apprehension about the way the Holy Spirit seemed to come to the disciples. The Bible uses imagery to describe the indescribable: it is not saying that the Spirit came with the destructive power of fire. Nor is this how many Christians experience it today.

Symbols: The Bible uses a great deal of symbolic language to try to convey ideas and 'pictures' hard to describe in ordinary terms. A symbol is a sign that evokes a response. It may be a physical image, such as the cross: or it may be an abstract image, such as a colour.

The Lord's Supper: The Last Supper shared by Jesus and the disciples before his death was the Passover Meal, celebrated by the Jewish people to this day to remember their deliverance from slavery in Egypt. In the framework of this meal, Jesus introduced another special meal – this time to remember his death for his followers. He used the bread and wine – integral parts of the Passover meal – and gave them new meaning. At first, the early Christians ate this in each others' houses as part of a meal enjoyed together.

Jewish Leaders: Please see the notes on p. 64.

Conversation

A. Christians believe that the Holy Spirit is a real but invisible friend. Can you think of any times when a Christian would be especially glad to know that he or she had such a friend?

B. Why did the disciples need the Holy Spirit? What was his job?

C. When the Holy Spirit came to the disciples, he seemed like a wind and fire. Sometimes in the Bible, he is seen as a dove. What does each of these symbols tell us about the Holy Spirit?

Reflection

When persecution started, it seemed that Jesus' plans were going wrong. But the persecution actually helped to spread the message about Jesus. Have there been times in your life when things seemed to go wrong, but really worked out better than ever? What should we remember from these things to help us in the future?

SIXTEEN

THE SUCCESSFUL FAILURE!

PETER - A LIFE OF CONTRASTS

Read about the life of our great leader!
- Thrill to the excitement as he walks on water
- Panic with him as he nearly drowns
- Rejoice with him as the sick are healed
- Despair with him as he runs away
- Admire his impetuous courage, and sympathise with his terror.

Never revealed before: the moving details of his life as a disciple and as an apostle.

What people have said about this book :

* ***'An honest account, well written'*** *James*
* ***'It brought back many events to me very vividly'*** *John*
* ***'If God could use this headstrong, ignorant fisherman, then there's hope for all of us'*** *A synagogue teacher*

Questions

1. When did Peter begin to sink?

2. What was the special job Jesus gave to the disciples?

3. How do you think Peter felt after his failures? Did Jesus give up on him?

Activity

Think about the main events of Peter's life: his calling by Jesus; his attempt to walk on the water; his statement that Jesus was the Messiah; his defence of Jesus in the garden; his denial that he knew Jesus; his private meeting with Jesus; his special job and his behaviour after Pentecost; his change of name. Design a front cover for the book described at the beginning of this section, using your intepretation of one or more of these events.

NOTE: The opinions of the synagogue teacher and of John and James are, of course, made up.

The Successful Failure!

Jesus' disciples travelled with him for years. They watched as he performed many wonderful miracles. They listened as he taught crowds of people. They listened as he taught just them. All the time, Jesus was preparing them for their great task, for they were to take the message of his love to other people, so that, gradually, the whole world heard about him.

Their strongest leader was Peter. But he was just an ordinary man. His life with Jesus was a series of triumphs and disasters. He was impetuous, rushing into things and thinking afterwards – often when it was too late! He was brave – very brave: but sometimes he panicked when he thought about the danger he was in.

One day, he was out fishing on the Sea of Galilee with some of the other disciples. They had left Jesus praying alone in the hills. Now, they were struggling to row against the strong wind. Suddenly, one of them saw Jesus – walking towards them on the water!

'Lord!' shouted Peter. 'Let me come to you!'

And Jesus said, 'Come!'

Eagerly, Peter climbed out of the boat – and stood firm on the water! Keeping his eyes on Jesus' face, he walked towards him! But then he realised how strong the wind was, and looked round nervously to see if the waves were going to wash over him. Immediately, he began to sink! Jesus reached out his hand and held him firmly. 'You should have believed in me,' he told Peter. 'You know I can keep you safe!'

Soon after this, Jesus asked his disciples, 'What are people saying about me? Who do they think I am?' They told him that people thought he must be one of their great leaders from the past. 'And who do you think I am?' he said.

Peter answered firmly. 'You are the Christ, the one we have waited for, God's own Son.'

Jesus smiled at him. 'Yes, Peter. God himself has chosen you specially and has told you this. From now on, you will be called "the rock", for my church will be built on the rock of your strength and teaching.'

But Peter did not always get things right! Jesus began to explain to his disciples that he would die soon. Peter interrupted! 'Never, Lord!' he shouted confidently. 'I will never let that happen!'

Jesus was disappointed. 'You are no help to me, talking like that,' he told him. 'I tell you that I have to die. You are thinking like a man, and not trying to understand God's plan.'

Did Peter listen to this? On the terrible night when soldiers came to arrest Jesus in the Garden of Gethsemane, Peter attacked one of them! Jesus had to tell him off again: 'There is no need to defend me. This has to happen. It is part of God's plan.'

The other disciples fled, but Peter followed Jesus as they took him away. And then happened the worst thing in his life so far. When some people recognised him as a follower of Jesus, in his terror he denied it. And when

he heard the cock crowing, he remembered that Jesus had said he would do just this before cock-crow – and he was heartbroken.

After Jesus' death, Peter must have felt that everything was over. He had let Jesus down, and had not even been able to say sorry. But, soon after he had risen, Jesus came to Peter, and they were able to talk together privately. Then, later, when Jesus met the disciples for breakfast on the shore, he showed Peter that he had forgiven him, and that he still had that special job for him – as leader and carer of his people.

Later, Peter stepped forward as their natural leader, just as Jesus had said he would.

(This story can be found throughout the four Gospels and in the Acts of the Apostles.)

Background Information

Names of Peter: Peter's given name was Simon. After his confession that Jesus was the Christ, Jesus said that he would now be called Peter, meaning 'rock', for, Jesus explained, 'on this rock I will build my church'. (Matthew 16:18)

Conversation

A. Look at the main events in Peter's life which are described in this story. What would Peter have learned about himself and about Jesus from each of these?

B. Would Peter's failures have made him a stronger or a weaker leader?

C. Discuss what Jesus meant when he called Peter the 'rock'. (Peter's name was originally Simon. Jesus actually changed his name to Peter, which means 'rock'.)

Reflection

Peter was not perfect! None of the disciples was. But Jesus chose them and trusted them to spread the message about him. We do not have to be perfect before we can help other people. We can start straightaway. We cannot expect ourselves to be perfect, either! Like Peter, we will make mistakes sometimes.

SEVENTEEN

FRIEND OR FOE?

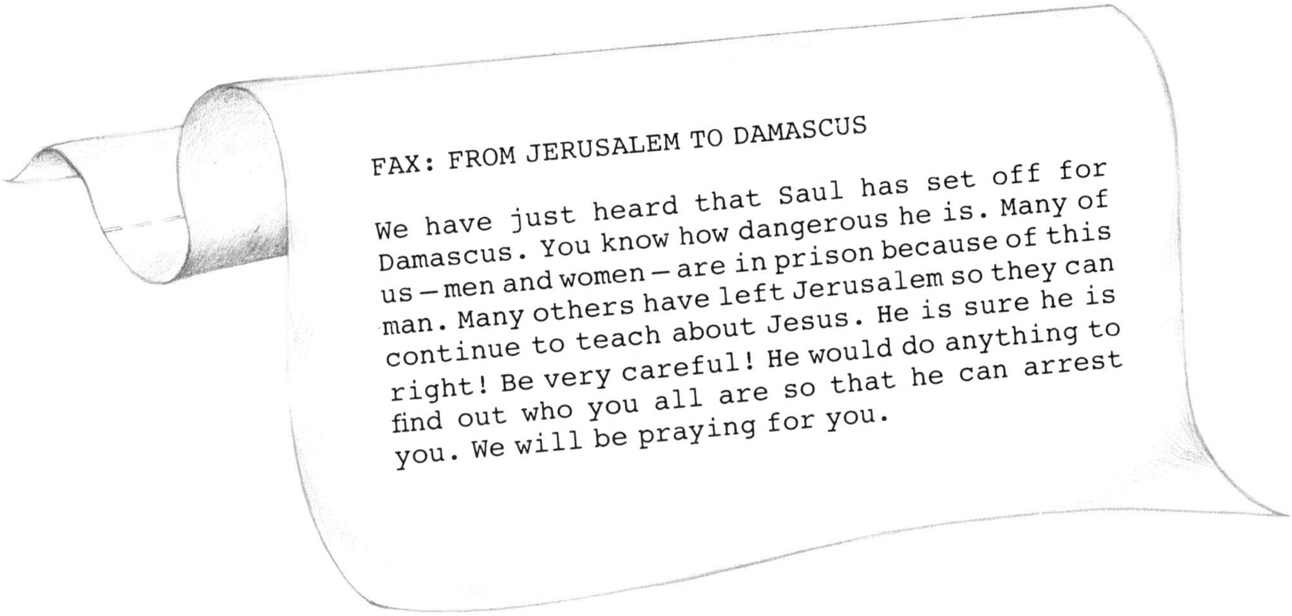

FAX: FROM JERUSALEM TO DAMASCUS

We have just heard that Saul has set off for Damascus. You know how dangerous he is. Many of us – men and women – are in prison because of this man. Many others have left Jerusalem so they can continue to teach about Jesus. He is sure he is right! Be very careful! He would do anything to find out who you all are so that he can arrest you. We will be praying for you.

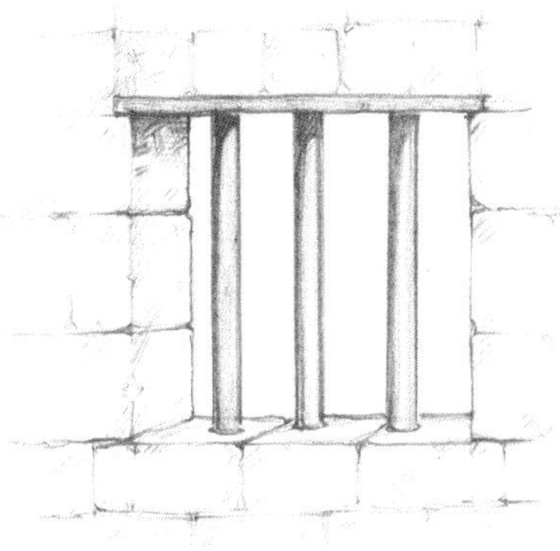

Questions

1. Why had Saul come to Damascus?

2. Why had Stephen been killed?

3. What happened to Saul on the way to Damascus?

Activity

Write another fax back to the Christians in Jerusalem who sent the first one. This one could be from Ananias, or you could make up a person. Tell the Christians in Jerusalem about Saul in Damascus.

Friend or Foe?

Saul crouched down in the great basket as it swung and rocked its way down the town wall of Damascus, lowered as smoothly as possible by his friends as they watched anxiously above. All was quiet: the guards had not heard them. The basket hit the ground with a slight thud. Saul clambered out, waved his thanks to his friends, and set off on the long walk back to Jerusalem, taking care to stay out of sight of the guards on the gate.

'This is not how I expected to be leaving Damascus!' he said to himself. 'I expected to ride out in style, with a crowd of Christian prisoners in tow. Instead, I am leaving in secret, saved by those very Christians, rescued from the Jewish leaders I was going to work with! They would have killed me if they'd found me, and been pleased to do it now that I'm a Christian – just as I was satisfied when Stephen was killed.'

He thought back to that day when he had watched Stephen die. Stephen was a Christian, a member of the new church that Saul hated. 'I was so sure they were wrong, and that Jesus was an imposter, a fake. I was determined to arrest all of them, and persuade them that they were wrong. Yes, and have them killed too if they wouldn't agree with me!' So he had left Jerusalem to carry on his work in Damascus.

But something happened on the way. Jesus himself spoke to Saul! A great light blinded him and he heard Jesus' voice. He came to believe that all he had heard about Jesus was true, and he became his follower. God had sent one of the Christians, Ananias, to Saul. Ananias had been horrified! He knew all about Saul! But he wanted to obey God, so he went to Saul – and found that Saul was now a Christian too, just like him! Saul smiled as he walked on through the night, thinking of his new friends in Damascus. Soon all the Christians there knew that Saul had joined them. He had told the other Jews about Jesus too, but their leaders were furious: how dare Saul turn against them like this? So Saul's new friends had smuggled him out of the town.

But when he arrived in Jerusalem, the Christian leaders were not sure it was safe to meet him. 'What if it's all a trick?' they muttered.

Barnabas spoke up. He described how Saul had met Jesus. 'He taught the people about Jesus,' he said, 'and nearly died as a result. God has chosen him: we have nothing to fear.'

So Saul was accepted as a leader. He began to travel from town to town to tell people about Jesus. And in many of these places new churches began as people learned from him about Jesus' love for them. Later, he wrote many letters to these churches, to teach and encourage them. We still have these letters today: Christians still read them and learn from them.

Saul's life was not easy. Travel was difficult then, and sometimes dangerous. He was often cold and hungry, and was shipwrecked three times. Many of the powerful men in the towns did not want Saul to teach about Jesus. They tried to stop him, just as he had tried to stop the Christians in Jerusalem and Damascus. They imprisoned him and whipped him. He survived riots and being pelted with stones. In the end, he spent long months under arrest. But he never stopped teaching about Jesus.

'None of these things matters at all,' he said. 'All that matters is that Jesus loves me and that I tell others about his love for them.'

(This story is taken from various episodes in the Book of Acts and the Epistles. These are the main references: Acts 6:8–12; 7:54–8:1; 9:1–31; 2 Corinthians 11:16–33; Philippians 3:8.)

Background Information

Saul: Saul was a Jew of some standing, and was highly regarded in Jerusalem. The opponents of Jesus' followers saw him as one of their main representatives as they tried to eliminate the Christians. The persecution in Jerusalem, which reached a new level with the death of Stephen, resulted in fact in the more rapid spread of the Gospel as many Christians left the capital to find freedom to teach elsewhere. Saul was commissioned by the authorities to go to Damascus to arrest any Christians he could find there. Saul was a Roman citizen, and as such was exempt from the floggings he later received from the Jews, but he accepted them as a Jew. In the same way, he could have avoided the floggings meted out to him by the Romans. He had studied under the finest teachers of the time. But all of his advantages meant nothing to him, in comparison with the importance of the message about God's love.

We now usually know him by the Roman form of his name, Paul.

The Jewish leaders: It should be pointed out to the children that not all of the Jews opposed Jesus. Jesus himself and most of his followers were Jews. The persecution was some Jews against some Jews, not all Jews against Christians.

Conversation

A. When the Jewish leaders in Damascus heard that Saul had become a Christian, they reacted with anger. Why?

B. When the Christians in Jerusalem heard the same news, they reacted with fear. Why?

C. Who spoke up for Saul in Jerusalem? What did he say to prove that Saul had really changed?

Reflection

The Christians in Damascus and Barnabas in Jerusalem proved their friendship by their actions or by speaking up for Saul. Do we do the same or find it easier to say nothing when we see misunderstanding or fear?

APPENDIX

ASSEMBLY IDEAS

KING IN A STABLE

Theme: Jesus' Birth.

You will need:

Two scripts – one for a child to read as Mary, and one for a child to read as a modern mother.
Simple costume for Mary: just a headdress would do.
Two dolls as babies. (One can be wrapped in swaddling-bands, made from strips of cloth, wrapped round a blanket around the baby.)
(Alternatively, a real 'new mum' may be willing to take part: she would need to alter the script accordingly.)

1. Discuss with the children the preparations our families make for an expected baby, mentioning such things as the buying or preparing of a cot and clothes. Talk also about deciding where the baby will be born, and about the help the mother will need during the birth and afterwards. How will a mother know how to look after her first baby? Emphasise the joy felt at the birth of a baby: all babies are special to their families!

2. Introduce the idea of Christmas being a celebration of the birth of a baby who was special to a lot of people. Christians believe that special baby was God's Son. But he was born in very strange surroundings.

3. Either: Choose two children to read the scripts. (A chance to read them through earlier would be useful, if possible. They can, of course, be easily adapted to the children's ability.) While dressing the children, explain who they are – Mrs Brown from Green Avenue and Mary from Palestine. Choose the child to play Mary with care. Explain that 'Mary' will convey Christians' understanding of Jesus.

Or: Introduce your visitor, thanking her for her time. Tell the children that she is going to tell them some facts about her baby.

4. Listen to the scripts.

5. These two babies had very different births! Mary had probably prepared many things at home ready for her baby. She had family and friends at home who would have looked after her and welcomed Jesus. But she had to leave her home because she and Joseph had to go to Bethlehem to have their names registered so that the Romans knew how many people could pay tax-money to them.

6. So Jesus was born into an ordinary, poor family, in a strange town and in a borrowed shelter. When the angel first told Mary that she was going to have a baby, he said, 'He will be great and will be called the Son of the Most High . . . and he will reign for ever.'

Prayer

Dear God, Thank you that you sent your Son to live in a family just like our families. Thank you that he knows what it is like to grow up in a family. Amen.

Music Suggestion

'See amid the winter snow', *Junior Praise*, comp. by P. Horrobin and G. Leavers (Marshall Pickering '86).
'See him lying on a bed of straw', *Junior Praise*, as above.
'Mary's child,' *Praise God Together*, comp. by M. Old (S.U. '88).
'The Shepherds,' *Sing-Song-Roundabout: Christmas*, comp. by B. Piper and F. Cooke (Longman '86).

Suggested Scripts

A MOTHER

I thought I was pregnant, so I went to see my doctor. S/he told me when my baby would be born.
I bought a new cot for my baby and some clothes. My friends gave me a lot of things I needed, and knitted ten pairs of mittens!
We decorated a bedroom ready for the baby.
My baby was born in a hospital.
S/he slept in a cot there.
There were doctors and nurses and midwives at the hospital to look after us.
When I went home, I had a lot of help from my family and friends.
My baby's name is   and his/her father is

MARY

An angel came to tell me I was having a baby.
I made some swaddling-bands out of an old piece of cloth. A friend gave me an old blanket for my baby. I used some of it to make a hammock for him.
My baby was born in a stable. He slept in a trough.
There were no doctors or nurses to look after us.
None of my family and friends were there to help me except for Joseph.
My baby's name is Jesus and his father is God.

CHRISTMAS PRESENTS!

Theme: Christmas Presents!

You will need:

Pieces of card on which to write
Felt tips

1. Talk about Christmas presents. Who likes to receive them? Who likes to give them? Sometimes, presents can be invisible: talk about the things we can do to help people: what about kindness or love? Caring and things like washing, cooking, etc.? Are these gifts too?

2. Let's look at the presents that were given at the first Christmas. Some of them are well-known: but some need thinking about.

3. Tell the story of Jesus' birth, the shepherds, and the wise men, pausing after the appropriate passages to ask:

'What did Mary and Joseph give to Jesus?' (love, protection, a family, warmth, etc.)
'What did the shepherds give to Jesus?' (obedience, worship.)
'What did the wise men give to Jesus?' (worship, gold, etc.)

(If time is short, the people concerned can just be mentioned, instead of the story being told.) Write each answer on a piece of card and choose children to hold them up. (You could have these children dressed as the characters: just headdresses would suffice.)

4. Christians believe that God gave the world a very special Christmas present that first Christmas. What do you think it was?

Prayer

Thank you Father God that you gave your Son at the first Christmas. Help us to remember that we can give to others in many different ways, at Christmas and at any time.

or Reflection

Why do we give presents to other people? Why do they give them to us? Sometimes the thought that has gone into a present, or the work, is even more pleasing than the present itself!

Music Suggestions

'A Song Was Heard at Christmas', *Praise God Together*, comp. M. Old (S.U. '88).
'The Wise Men', *Sing-Song-Roundabout: Christmas*, B. Piper and F. Cooke (Longman, '86).

LOST IN THE CITY?

Theme: Latest score – Parents 5 Children 2.

You will need:

Copies of the scripts below, if necessary

1. Read the title of the assembly. What does it sound like? (some sort of sporting contest). Sometimes, getting on with our parents seems like a continual match – or even like a series of pitched battles! We live very closely with people who are not completely like us, with their own likes and dislikes, and their own opinions about things. No wonder we sometimes fall out and argue! Listen to these short conversations between children and their mother or father.

2. (These can be read by you or by children.)

Father and son
What time will you be home tonight?
You don't trust me, do you!

Daughter and mother
Mum, I've run out of clean school blouses!
You know how busy I've been. Can't you do one?
I was going to!

Mother and daughter
You look very nice today.
Oh, I usually look a mess, do I?

Mother and son
Do you want some more stew?
No, thank you, Mum.
You don't like it, do you!

3. These sound like the beginning of arguments. How could the people in each one have prevented this? Talk about such things as listening to everything carefully, and giving each other time to speak and explain: misunderstandings and misinterpretations: remembering if the other person has particular problems or worries at the moment. Point out that both children and parents 'go off the deep end' in these examples!

4. Ask what sort of things annoy children about parents, and vice versa. Point out that some of these things are actually good things – such as protectiveness – or inevitable. They can be carried to excess, though.

5. Jesus met difficulties, too, living in Mary and Joseph's family. Tell the story of Jesus in the Temple; Mary and Joseph failed to understand where Jesus' loyalties lay: he had to think about what God wanted, as well as what they wanted.

6. Life at home would be easier if both 'sides' could try to understand the other more, and to make allowances for behaviour that is due to the differences between them or due to concern for each other – but this is difficult at times!

(N.B. Keep this non-threatening and impersonal. Point out at the beginning that only general comments are allowed.)

Prayer

Father, we all have to live with other people. Help us to try to see things from their point of view – to ask why they are behaving like this. Help us to be patient with each other.

Music Suggestion

'Amen', *Alleluya!* chosen by D. Gadsby and J. Hoggarth (A. and C. Black Ltd., London, '91).
'Lord of all hopefulness', *Sing to God* comp. M. Old and E. Stephenson (S.U. '86).

'THIS IS MY SON!'

Theme: A proper wash!

1. How many times have you heard those words: 'Have a proper wash this time!' We don't have any real excuse for not washing properly in this country! We have plenty of water, and the water is clean. We don't have to work hard, carrying every drop of water into the house. Have any of you been on a camping or caravanning holiday when you did have to carry all your water? What did you think of it? Perhaps some of you have had your water cut off in the past, and had to fetch your water then. Imagine having to do that all the time!

2. In some countries, of course, that is just what they have to do. And very often it is the children who have to do it. Listen to this story.

In a small village, in a hilly part of India, there was a pond of water. It was not very large, and it was not very clean. The water ran down the hillsides into the pond when it rained: but it did not rain very often! The dogs drank from the pond, and rolled in its water: and the oxen drank too, stirring up the mud with their hooves. The women of the village washed the clothes in it, beating them on the flat rocks they had put in the water. And every day, the women and children walked down from the village with their empty water jars, filled them in the pond, and returned, carefully balancing them on their heads.

But the people of the village were worried. So many children were ill! Some had even died. 'Why is this happening to us?' they asked each other. One of the village elders looked down at the pond from their meeting place under the tree.

'Perhaps it is the pond,' he said. 'Look at it! The oxen have trampled all around it and there is rubbish everywhere. We must clean it up!'

So next day the whole village worked hard. They cut down the shrubs growing close to the water. They made a path down to the water, and trod stones into it, so that it would not get too muddy again. They even planted some flowering plants round it. They tried to stop the animals going into the water. But it soon became obvious that they had not succeeded. The children grew worse: and now adults were ill, too.

'But what else can we do?' they asked. 'This is the only water we have. We have to drink it.'

Finally, they asked their Government to send a scientist out to them, to tell them what needed doing. He examined the water, taking samples throughout the day. 'This water is not fit to drink,' he told them. 'It is making your children ill.'

The villagers explained that they already knew this! But they had done all they could. The visitor said that he could help. He would bring equipment to drain the pond. They would reline it with layers of gravel and sand and stones, to stop the soil mixing into the water. A ditch would be dug above the spring on the hillside, so that the rainwater could no longer wash soil into it. And they would build proper steps going down into the water, so that they did not trample the banks into mud. They would build a fence around it to stop the animals. 'And we have the money too, to pay for all this,' he ended.

The villagers had to work hard on the new pond. But soon it was ready, and they had what they needed – clean water.

3. The villagers altered the appearance of the pond. It looked better. But nothing had changed really. The water itself needed changing. Very often, we do not like the way we act. We want to change ourselves. We can make ourselves seem better by what we do. But we can't change ourselves inside. Christians believe that Jesus can change people. He can help people to behave differently, and to be different.

4. Introduce the idea of baptism – or refer to any work already done on this. If time allows, tell the story of Jesus' baptism. Explain that many different churches still use baptism today, as a sign of a new relationship with God. John the Baptist and Jesus both spoke of baptism as being for the 'forgiveness of sins'. This does not mean that the actual water 'cleans' people from their sins. Baptism is used as a picture, to show that God has already forgiven the person's sins: he has already 'washed' them.

Prayer

Thank you Father that you can help us to change – on the inside – and that you want to help us.

Music Suggestions

'Jesus was baptised in Jordan', *Praise God Together*, comp. M. Old (S.U. '88).
'I am the way, the truth and the life', *Junior Praise*, comp. P. Horrobin and G. Leavers (Marshall Pickering '86).

REAL FRIENDS?

Theme: What makes a real friend?

You will need:

Felt-tips/pens
The outlines of two children on separate pieces of paper
Strips of paper with 'A friend is someone who . . .' written on them, with space to add a child's comment to add to one figure
Strips of paper with 'A friend is not someone who . . .' written on them, with space to add a child's comment, to add to the other figure
Blutak or similar

1. Introduce the theme of friendship: what makes a real friend?

a) If the children have already done the work in class, say they have been looking at what made Jesus' disciples 'good friends' to him.

b) Show the strips with 'A friend is someone who . . .' on them, and ask the children for appropriate endings. If the others agree an ending is useful, write it on and let the child who suggested it stick it on the first figure.

2. Repeat this, using the 'A friend is not someone who . . .' strips, and the second outline.

3. Read out the 'facts' you have collected about friends. Here are some of the 'facts' the Bible gives us about friends:

'A friend loves at all times.' Proverbs 17:17
'A friend sticks closer than a brother.' Proverbs 18:24
'A friend may hurt you in order to help you, but an enemy only wants to hurt you.' Proverbs 27:6

Discuss what these mean.

Reflection

Read through the sentences on the 'good friend' figure or listen while they are read out to you. Do you think you are a 'good friend'?
Now read or listen to the 'not a good friend' sentences. Do any of them fit you? Think how you could be a better friend to your friends.

Music Suggestion

'Father, I place into your hands . . .' *Junior Praise*, comp. by P. Horrobin and G. Leavers (Marshall Pickering '86).
'Jesus is a friend of mine', ibid.
'Jesus went a-walking', *Many Ways to Praise*, comp. by S. Sayers (Palm Tree Press '86).

WHO IS THIS MAN?

Theme: 'Give us a clue!'

You will need:

Various 'clues' to different people, depending upon which you choose, and some way of concealing them.
Cards with statements about Jesus' actions before the storm episode. Select some from:
He healed Peter's mother-in-law.
He healed the centurion's servant without even seeing him.
He taught great crowds of people.
He told them he was the one sent by God to tell people how to become God's friends.
He healed a man who couldn't walk.

1. We are going to play an identity game – a 'guess my job' game. Explain that you have three clues to somebody's job to show them. You will start with the most difficult clue. (This can be played with two selected teams if preferred, instead of on a 'hands up' basis.) Produce the clues one at a time, for a selection of characters. (Some possiblities are: teacher, musician, doctor, dinner helper, shopkeeper, lollipop person, bus driver, police officer, fire officer, mother, carer. Toy versions of the tools of their trades would be useful!)

2. Once, Jesus told off his disciples because they had not realised who he was from the clues they had been given. Tell the story of the storm.

3. Jesus said that the disciples had received plenty of clues about the type of person he was. They should have known that there was no need to panic. Here are some of the clues that they had already received. Show them some of the statements about Jesus, saying what each showed the disciples about Jesus.

Prayer

Father, please help us to be open to new ideas, and to ask ourselves questions as the disciples did when they met Jesus.

Music Suggestions

'Put your hand in the hand' (first verse), *Alleluya!*, chosen by D. Gadsby and J. Hoggarth (A. and C. Black Ltd., London, '91).
'Power of Jesus', *Sing-Song-Roundabout: Bible Stories of Jesus* by B. Piper and F. Cooke (Longman).
'With Jesus in the boat', *Junior Praise*, comp. by P. Horrobin and G. Leavers (Marshall Pickering, '86).

(NOTE: an alternative could be to produce clues relating to famous people, or even to people within the school.)

'IT'S TOO LATE!'

Theme:'But do you really believe it?'

You will need:

Children to act out the Bible story. They need not be familiar with the story as you will be telling the story as they follow it.

1. Introduce the difference between believing something and actually being prepared to act upon your belief. Read the following story.

Two men were talking during their coffee break. 'Are you still doing that parachute jump for Red Nose Day, Paul?' asked Steve.

'Yes. It seemed a good thing to do. I did a lot of jumps when I was in the Marines, and I've done a full refresher course down at the airfield.'

'How much have you been sponsored for, then?' his friend asked.

'A lot! People are always glad to sponsor someone else! It makes them feel they are doing some good without having to make much of an effort.'

Steve nodded vigorously. 'I agree! Some people just won't put themselves out at all, will they? Not even for a good cause like this!'

'What are you doing then?' asked Paul.

Steve began to study his coffee cup very closely! 'Er ... nothing, actually,' he admitted.

'Why don't you join me?' Paul suggested. 'There's time for you to train, and we could double our sponsor money if we jumped in tandem.'

Steve looked uncomfortable. 'Well ... I'm not very good at that sort of thing,' he said.

'You don't need to be. I'd look after you. You'd be perfectly safe.' Seeing that his friend still looked doubtful, Paul added, 'Don't you trust me?'

'Of course I do!' Steven answered. 'I know how experienced you are. I know you wouldn't put me in danger.'

'But you still don't want to do it?' Paul persisted.

'No,' admitted Steve quietly. 'I daren't!'

2. Point out that Steve believed that Paul would be safe and would be able to look after both of them – but he wasn't willing to commit himself and his safety into his friend's hands. The people in this Bible story believed Jesus could help them, and were willing to act upon this.

3. Tell the story of Jairus' daughter and the woman who touched Jesus. Children could act this out while you tell it, if appropriate.

4. Christians believe that Jesus did not perform miracles to create a sensation. He looked for people who had faith in him, who believed that he could help them and who acted on this belief. Who were these people in this story?

Reflection

People like to feel that they can trust each other. It makes them feel safe and secure. Christians believe that Jesus is completely trustworthy: he will never let them down. Think about people who trust you. How would they feel if you let them down?

Music Suggestions

'Rise and live', *Sing-Song-Roundabout: Bible Stories of Jesus,* by B. Piper and F. Cooke (Longman) (no date available).
'Come to Jesus, he's amazing', *Junior Praise,* comp. by P. Horrobin and G. Leavers (Marshall Pickering, '86).

EVERYBODY WELCOME!

Theme: 'How much are you worth?'

You will need:

A selection of articles of differing value. It is useful if some at least are in 'pairs', with one of each pair being far more valuable than the other because it is made/decorated, etc. by somebody famous for that work. (For instance, some pottery or prints of paintings.) At least one object should carry value because of its rarity (this might be the same as the above). One object could be valuable only to you – sentimental value because of its maker.
Price labels for these objects – blank and/or filled in – see below.
Price labels for a child, one with £0 on and one reading 'Priceless'.
Felt-tips

1. Talk about the interest in antiques and programmes such as 'The Antiques Roadshow', etc. What about carboot sales and secondhand shops? Why are people interested in these? Everyone hopes that they, too, will find a treasure in disguise! How good would the children be if they went treasure hunting? Let's find out!

2. Show the objects to the children, with a brief description of each. Do not give away their value, but do tell them what each is made of.

3. Let the children guess how much the objects are worth. This can be done two ways, depending on how much help you feel they need: let them guess entirely by themselves, and then label the objects accordingly; or have your estimated prices already on the labels, and let them assign them to the objects. You can select a group to do this, or ask for 'offers'.

4. Reveal and attach the true prices, after telling them how accurate they have been. Point out that some objects may appear very similar, but that the name attached to one makes it far more valuable. Other objects are valuable because of their rarity.

5. How much do you think people are worth? Christians believe that we are made by God, and that this makes us very valuable. They also believe that we are valuable because each of us is unique: there is no one like us, never has been anyone like us and never will be. So how valuable are we? Choose a child – (carefully!) – and say that Christians believe this child is priceless! Discuss the meaning of this: use the £0 label and explain it does not mean this. Cross it out! Relabel the child 'Priceless' and explain what it means.

Prayer

Thank you Father that we are all different and that, to you, we are all of great value.

Music Suggestion

'Whether you're one', *Junior Praise*, comp. by P. Horrobin and G. Leavers (Marshall Pickering, '86).

'Hundreds and thousands', *Sing to God*, comp. by M.V. Old and E.M. Stephenson (S.U. '86).
'Let the children come', *Sing-Song Roundabout: Bible Stories of Jesus*, by B. Piper and F. Cooke (Longman, no date on book).

WHO WILL HELP?

Theme: 'What is a neighbour?'

You will need:

Instead of the Proverbs being read, they could be written out beforehand by the children.
If the story has already been covered in class, it could be acted out as part of the assembly, with or without a commentary.

1. How many of you have heard of or watch 'Neighbours' on television? What/who is it about? Bring out the fact that it is about the people living on one street only. This is what people usually mean by neighbours.

2. In the Bible, we read that we should love our neighbour in the same way as we love ourselves. Someone asked Jesus who his neighbour was, and Jesus told this story to show him.

3. Read or act the story of the Good Samaritan.

4. Ask/explain that our neighbour is anyone who needs help or who helps us when we need help.

5. The Bible gives us advice on how we can look after our neighbours. Here are some examples.

'Do not cheat your neighbour or rob him.' Leviticus 19:13
'Do not do anything that puts your neighbour's life in danger.' Leviticus 19:16
'Do not take revenge on your neighbour or bear a grudge against him.' Leviticus 19:18
'The man who hates his neighbour is doing wrong.' Proverbs 14:21
'A man who lies about his neighbour does as much damage as a club or a sword or a sharp arrow.' Proverbs 25:18
'Each of you must stop telling lies and must speak truthfully to your neighbour.' Ephesians 4:25

Reflection

Think about how you like other people to treat you. Then think about how you treat other people. Is there much difference?

Music suggestion

'Cross over the road' *Praise God together*, comp. M. Old (S.U. '88).
'A Samaritan on a lonely road', *Sing to God*, comp. M. Old and E. Stephenson (S.U. '86).

THE FATHER WHO WAITED

Theme: Jesus the Shepherd.

You will need:

Copies of the script – or this can just be read

1. Jesus wanted people to understand what God was like. He particularly wanted them to realise that God loved them and cared for them. When he was teaching, he often used stories to explain what he meant, and he used the things the people knew about to illustrate his teaching. In the parable of the lost son, he used the image of God as a loving, forgiving father. God is also represented as a caring shepherd. Listen to this conversation.

2. Sheep 1: Hello.
Sheep 2: Hello.

1: Do you come here often?
2: No. This is the first time. It's nice here, isn't it?
1: Yes. It's one of our favourite spots. Our shepherd often brings us here. The water's just right – good and fresh, but not flowing fast enough to be dangerous.
2: Mmm. . . The grass is good too – very tender.

Silence as they both eat.

1: You by yourself, then? Where's your shepherd?
2: Oh, him! Could be anywhere. Probably asleep. I do like this grass. My friend would love it here.
1: Your friend? Is he here, then? (looking round)
2: She.
1: Pardon?
2: She. She's a she.
1: Oh. I see.
2: No, she's not round here. Last time I saw her, a wolf was after her. Up there in the hills.
1: Oh dear.
2: Oh, I think she'd escape. She's a good runner. Has to be. We all have to be!
1: What about your shepherd? Where was he when this happened?
2: I don't know. Could have been anywhere. Asleep, probably.
1: I see.
2: Well, I think I'll just have a drink, then I'll get back to my family – if I can find them! 'Bye!
1: 'Bye! Look after yourself!
2: Have to, mate. No one else does!

3. This is based on an Old Testament poem in which King David said that God looked after him like a shepherd. (If time permits, you can discuss how a shepherd

looked after his sheep in those days.) Jesus also said that he is the Good Shepherd: he looks after his people all the time. What were the differences between the 'good' and the 'bad' shepherds in the sketch? Christians believe that Jesus provides all they need. He leads them, showing them what they should do. He never leaves them. They also believe that he died for people, just as a good shepherd risks his own life to protect his sheep.

Reflection

Jesus described himself as the Good Shepherd. This means that he cares for people. Think of what would happen to a flock of sheep who had a 'bad' shepherd.

Music Suggestions

'A father's love', *Sing-Song-Roundabout: Bible stories of Jesus*, by B. Piper and F. Cooke (Longman, no date).
'You can't stop God from loving you', *Sing to God*, comp. M. Old and E. M. Stephenson (S.U. '86).

'AND NOW SAY THANK YOU!'

Theme: 'Now say thank you!'

You will need:

If the sketch is acted out, two copies of it will be needed, and something to represent the gift.

1. Do you ever get fed-up being told what to say? Listen to/watch this short sketch.

Aunt: Hello, Jan. Look what I've brought you! (*She hands over the gift. Jan begins to unwrap it.*)
Aunt: Well? Is it the one you wanted? (*Impatiently.*)
Jan: Yes! I've got the whole set now!
Aunt: Well? What do you say?
Jan: (*busy examining the gift*) Pardon?
Aunt: (*angrily*) Right! Those who can't say thank you don't get the gift! (*She snatches back the gift.*)

2. Why did Jan lose the gift? Do you think she meant not to say thank you? Christians believe that as Jesus travelled around his country, he gave many gifts to people. Can you think of any? (Help them to list such things as sight, healing, health, life, time – or just tell them about these things.) I wonder how many people said thank you to him: and what happened if they didn't?

3. Tell the story of the ten lepers. At the end, point out or ask what happened to the nine who did not say thank you. Their gift was not withdrawn.

4. Christians believe that God is still like this today. He does not take away his gifts just because people do not say thank you for them. So why should people say thank you – to God or to anyone? Draw out the need to feel appreciated and to return thoughtfulness. Christians believe that God, too, likes us to show our enjoyment of his gifts.

Reflection

Think of something you enjoy that God or somone else has given you. Remember, gifts can be solid – like a computer game or chocolate – or something like time and care. Have you said thank you? What can you do about it if you haven't? How can you show that person that the gift was really appreciated?

Music Suggestions

'Thank you, Lord', *Praise God Together*, comp. by M. Old (S.U. '88).
'Who took fish and bread', *Junior Praise*, comp. P. Horrobin and G. Leavers (Marshall Pickering '86).

'BUT HE DOESN'T DESERVE IT!'

Theme: Change.

You will need:

Costumes for dressing up, or
Cards with names on them

1. Tell the children your name and describe briefly what sort of person you are. Mention such things as your job, your hobbies, what sort of holiday you enjoy.

2. Choose another name from the name-cards. Tell them you are now this person. Alternatively, dress up as someone else using the costumes.

3. Discuss with the children – has this really changed me? Am I still the same person or a different one?

4. Today's story is about a man who didn't change his name or his appearance. But he did change in another way!

Listen carefully, and tell me at the end of the story what did change about him.

5. Read or tell the story of Zacchaeus on p 55. (If this story has already been used with a class, they could now act it out instead of the teacher presenting it.)

Prayer

Dear God, sometimes we do or say things that we know are wrong. Please help us to remember that you can help us to change, just as you helped Zacchaeus. Amen.

Music Suggestion

'Father, I place into your hands. . .', *Junior Praise*, comp. by P. Horrobin and G. Leavers (Marshall Pickering '86).

DEAD!

Theme: We need to be sorry and to want to change, in order to be forgiven.

1. When we live and work and play with our families and friends, we often hurt or upset each other – on purpose or by accident. Ask the children for examples of times when we might need to say sorry. Explain that it is more difficult to forgive someone who is not sorry for what they have done.

2. But is saying sorry enough? (No answer needed yet!) Read the passage:

'Come in!' Mrs Wakefield called, and Lucy crept into the Headmistress' room. Mrs Wakefield looked up from her work. 'Not you again, Lucy!' she exclaimed.

'Yes,' Lucy whispered.

'What is it this time?' the teacher asked, laying down her pen and sighing.

'Well, Miss, you see, Miss, I was only trying to help, and I thought he was hungry so I . . . I . . .'

'Yes, Lucy,' Mrs. Wakefield prompted, 'you what?'

'Well, the hamster did look hungry. I mean, he hadn't been fed for hours, and I thought that I'd just give him a snack before we went for our dinner. So I opened the door, and . . .' Lucy stopped miserably.

'And you let him out?' suggested Mrs Wakefield.

Lucy started to cry. The teacher handed her a tissue: and then another one: and then another. 'I'm so sorry, Mrs Wakefield, really I am!' she sobbed.

The Headmistress shook her head, and smiled at the miserable little girl in front of her. 'Sit down, Lucy,' she said. 'Now, how many times have you been to see me this week?'

'Five,' Lucy replied.

'Yes. Once a day. And what was it you did wrong on Monday? Ah yes – you let the hamster out.'

'He was new and frightened,' Lucy explained. 'I wanted to help him.'

'I'm not sure that being chased by the united efforts of Mr Stone and 4B helped him at all – but never mind. And Tuesday? You decided the cage was dirty didn't you? Wednesday?'

'I was giving him more water, and yesterday I just wanted a cuddle with him.'

Mrs Wakefield stood up. 'Each day, you have let Houdini out, and he's had to be chased and recaptured. And each day you've come in here and used up a whole week's tissues, telling me how sorry you are.'

'But I am sorry – very sorry!' Lucy assured her.

'I know you are, dear, but it's not enough to be sorry. How does Mr Stone feel? He's very annoyed with you. Every day, he accepts your apology and every day you do it again! As well as saying sorry, you must try not to do it again. I want you to go back and promise you will try to keep your hands off Houdini. If you really are sorry, then you'll really mean it, and try to do it. Alright?'

'Yes, Mrs Wakefield, I won't do it again!' promised Lucy.

3. Discuss the idea of needing to change our behaviour when we ask for forgiveness. The cross reminds Christians that God forgives them and helps them to change when they know that they need this.

Prayer

Dear God, help us to remember that you are always ready to forgive us when we do the wrong thing. Thank you that you will help us not to make the same mistake again. Amen.

Music Suggestions

'Live, live, live', *Junior Praise*, comp. by P. Horrobin and G. Leavers (Marshall Pickering '86).
'He made the Stars to Shine', *Praise God Together*, comp. M. Old (S.U. '88).
'O, what a gift', ibid.

ALIVE!

Theme: Surprise! Surprise!

You will need:

Examples of seeds and bulbs
Bare winter twigs, if possible, and leafy twigs: use only safe shrubs and twigs cut in pruning
Two Easter eggs – the type with a hidden toy inside, one of which has a slip of paper inside the inner container, reading 'Jesus is alive!' (It is quite easy to open the egg along its 'join', insert the paper in the container, and reseal – or just rewrap as if sealed.)

1. Talk about spring as a time of new birth and of new beginnings for plants and animals. Show the seeds, etc. Point out how dead these appear to be, but how much life is really hidden inside them. Introduce Easter; what do you think of when it is mentioned? If it is around Easter, ask about Easter eggs hoped for or received.

2. Show the children the eggs you have. What is inside? They are called 'surprise' eggs. Why? Open one and show them the toy inside. Why do we have eggs at Easter? Link them with the idea of new life and new birth.

3. To Christians, Easter is very special. They believe that it is the sign of their new life as followers of Jesus, because they believe that at the first Easter, Jesus rose from the dead. He defeated death so that his followers could have a new kind of life, one that never ends.

4. The first followers of Jesus had a surprise at Easter, too. They had seen Jesus die. They were very unhappy. Then, suddenly, Jesus was there, with them. He was alive!

Let's open this other egg and see what is in it. Open it or let a child help you with it. Open the container, and show them the message. This is the really important part of Easter for Christians. This is the greatest surprise at Easter: Jesus is alive!

Prayer

Lord, it is good to receive – and eat – eggs at Easter! But help us to remember the real surprise of Easter.

Music Suggestions

'Resurrection shout', *Many Ways to Praise*, comp. S. Sayers (Palm Tree Press '86).
'O what a gift', *Praise God Together*, comp. M. Old (S.U. '88).

WHAT A CHANGE!

Theme: Sharing.

You will need:

Sweets (check for possible allergies in children chosen) – preferably in small bags or yoghurt pots
Placard reading, 'You must share!' Give this secretly to a child before the assembly begins.

1. Choose two children. Give one of them a few sweets. Explain they are not to be eaten now, but are his/hers to keep. Send him/her to sit down. Ask the other children, 'Do you think . . . will share those with friends? Does he/she have to? What does it depend on?' Bring out choice, liking, generosity.

2. Give the other child a few sweets. This time, things are different. We are changing the rules! Ask the 'secret' child to hold up the placard. What must . . . . . do now? What will make him/her share this time? (Don't let the child actually choose anyone to share with: this could be divisive! Either cancel the law by teacher's decree, or say he/she has to choose you.)

3. Introduce the early church and the way they shared everything. Read Acts 2:44, 45: 'The believers shared everything. They sold their belongings in order to give money and food to those who needed it.' (paraphrased) Why did they do this? They didn't have to do it! There was no law saying, 'You must share!' They did it because they knew God wanted them to, and because they themselves wanted to. They cared for each other and believed it was wrong for them to have plenty of money and food if others did not have enough.

4. What about today? There are many people who do not have enough in the world now. But others are very rich. There is nothing wrong in being rich! We are talking about sharing, not about giving everything away. What would happen if everyone began to share things more equally? What could make them do this? (Do not let the children feel guilty because they can do little to help. We have all suffered from the 'Eat that up, some people are starving,' syndrome! Instead, look for simple ways they can share and help others.)

Reflection

It is right for us to enjoy what we have! There is no need to feel guilty because someone else has not got it. But we do need to think about sharing. Sharing something may be difficult; but it can make things fairer. Can you start, in some small way, to share something today?

Music Suggestions

'It is the Holy Spirit's day', *Praise God Together*, comp. M. Old (S.U. '88).
'Someone's lonely, Lord', ibid.
'With the Father when the world began', *Sing to God*, comp. M. Old and E. Stephenson (S.U. '86).

THE SUCCESSFUL FAILURE

Theme: Peter – the successful failure.

You will need:

Pieces of card with Peter's 'titles' on them, to display to the children (see below)

1. Introduce Peter – one of the most important leaders of the early church. With God's help, he performed miracles, taught hundreds of people about God, and helped the church to spread all over the world. But – he didn't always get things right! We are going to look at some of the titles he could be given.

2. Give the titles, one at a time, to children to hold up. Give brief information about each one, as suggested. (Or fewer titles could be dealt with in greater detail.)

Simon – his real name was Simon.
Fisherman – he was a fisherman on the Sea of Galilee when Jesus asked him to become his disciple.
Disciple – this meant he travelled round with Jesus, learning from him all the time.
Walker on the Water – he once tried to join Jesus who was walking on the water of the Sea of Galilee. But as soon as he looked at the waves instead of at Jesus, he became a . . .
Drowning Man – but Jesus saved him!
'Truth Teller' – he was the first disciple to say that Jesus was the Messiah, God's special King.
Liar and Coward – he denied that he even knew Jesus when he thought he was in danger.
Hero – he tried to fight off the soldiers arresting Jesus.

3. So, Simon – or Peter – was a typical human – a mixture of good and bad things. Why did Jesus choose him as his special leader? Jesus knew just what Peter was like. He knew that Peter would let God use him and change him. Jesus changed his name from Simon to Peter, which means 'the rock'. What did he mean by calling him this? Discuss the solidity, strength, etc. of rock, and how Peter could share some of these qualities as a human.

Reflection

None of us is perfect. We should not be too proud of ourselves, believing we can do nothing wrong. But we should not be too discouraged, either! We are only human – we will get some things wrong! Christians believe that Jesus can help people to do more things right.

Music Suggestions

'Here comes Jesus', *Praise God Together,* comp. M. Old (S.U. '88).

'Peter and John went to pray', *Junior Praise,* comp. P. Horrobin and G. Leavers (Marshall Pickering '86).

FRIEND OR FOE?

Theme: What was important to Saul? What is important to us?

You will need:

A large set of classroom scales
Several small light objects, such as boxes. Each needs a piece of paper on it: each will represent one of the troubles Saul endured, such as shipwreck, hunger, etc. (These can be written on during the assembly or previously.)
A larger block which is noticeably heavier than the others put together. This will have 'Jesus' love for me and telling others about his love for them' written on it.
Felt tips

1. Ask the children what is the most important thing in their lives. They do not have to share their answers. Ask for a show of hands: how many chose something that makes them happy? Comment that sometimes we seem to have so many problems that we stop thinking about the good things.

2. Today's story is about a man who started off as an enemy of the first Christians, but who became their friend. Becoming a Christian caused him a lot of problems, but he never stopped thinking about the good things in his life.

3. Read the story about Saul.

4. (Talk about how the scales work if necessary.) Explain that we are going to find out what the most important thing was to Saul. We will put his problems in one side of the scales, and the good things in his life in the other. Ask the children to tell you the problems Saul met with as he travelled. (These could already be written on the smaller blocks, or could be added now.) As the children remember these, add the blocks to one pan on the scales.

5. These problems look very heavy. Saul must have felt unhappy with all these dragging him down. But let's see what he said about them. Read the story's last sentence again. Show them the block with this on and place it in the other side. Explain that these things were so important to Saul that they made the problems seem light to him. The message wasn't 'heavy' because he was happy when he was working for God.

Prayer

Dear God, sometimes we are miserable because our problems seem so big to us. Help us to remember that you care for us, and that many other people care for us too and will help us. Amen.

Music Suggestion

'The greatest thing in all my life is knowing you', *Junior Praise*, comp. by P. Horrobin and G. Leavers (Marshall and Pickering '86).
'Jesus' love is very wonderful', ibid.

Faith in History

Ideas for RE, History and Assembly in the Primary School

Margaret Cooling

Faith in History is

- Based on the history of Christianity
- For use with 7 to 12 year-olds
- Designed to encourage pupils to learn from the past
- Lavishly illustrated throughout

Faith in History refers to the Channel Islands; England; The Isle of Man; Northern Ireland; Scotland and Wales

Faith in History covers

- Romans, Saxons and Vikings
- Tudors and Stuarts
- Victorian Britain
- Britain since 1930
- Churches through the ages

Faith in History contains

- 54 different topics
- Background information for teachers
- Primary and secondary source material
- Practical activities for pupils
- Photocopiable elements
- An introduction examining important educational issues

'A fascinating, scholarly and practical resource for the non-specialist. Unlike so many books of this kind, this one allows everyone's point of view to be valued.'

Carol Craggs, Stevenson Junior School, Nottingham

'The topic generated great enthusiasm. Words used by the children included: fantastic, challenging, searching, interesting, fun, excellent, enjoyable.'

Joyce Round, Bierton C of E Combined School, Buckinghamshire

MARGARET COOLING is the author of a number of books on primary school religious education and assemblies and regularly leads INSET courses for teachers. She is employed by the Association of Christian Teachers and is based at Stapleford House Education Centre, Nottingham.

ISBN 0 86347 106 4
Eagle Publishing

Faith in History
Worksheets

Bringing History and RE Alive

Margaret Cooling

Faith in History Worksheet Packs

- are available as a complete set in four thematic packs
- present 52 different sheets each containing a number of activities
- are fully photocopiable and printed on durable card
- contain a variety of activities
- are suitable for individual, group or class use
- cover the following themes:

- ***Invaders and Settlers*** - from Roman Christian Faith and Christian Secret Signs to Viking Crosses and Churches

- ***Tudors and Stuarts*** - from the Bible and Pilgrim's Progress to Isaac Newton and The Plague at Eyam

- ***Victorian Britain*** - from The Cab Horse Charter and Factory Conditions to Victorian Churches

- ***Britain after 1930*** - from C S Lewis and Christians under Occupation to Modern Christian Music

Faith in History - complete pack	ISBN 0 86347 133 1
Invaders and Settlers (double length pack)	ISBN 0 86347 134 X
Tudors and Stuarts	ISBN 0 86347 135 8
Victorian Britain	ISBN 0 86347 136 6
Britain after 1930	ISBN 0 86347 137 4

Faith in History and ***Faith in History Worksheets*** when used together provide all the necessary resources to conduct 52 lively, complete lessons and assemblies.